CARBOLIC SMOKE BALL

Enjoy!

Charlie Henn

CARBOLICSMOKEBALL

One of America's great web sites.

(And now one of America's great books.)

FIRST CARBOLIC MEDIA EDITION, NOVEMBER 2008

Copyright © 2008 by The Hon. Judge Rufus Peckham

All rights reserved. Published in the United States by Carbolic Smoke Books,
a division of Carbolic Smoke Ball, LLC., Pittsburgh, Pennsylvania.

Printed in Canada by Transcontinental Printing.

Library of Congress Cataloging-in-Publication Data Available from Carbolic Books.

Carbolic ISBN # 978-0-615-25526-2

Book design and layout by Chad Hermann.

Cover art and illustrations by Timothy Stefko.

www.carbolicsmoke.com

CARBOLICSMOKEBALL

presents

The Hon. Judge Rufus Peckham

CARBOLICSMOKEBOOKS

A DIVISION OF CARBOLIC SMOKE BALL, LLC
PITTSBURGH, PA

For Carol, whose love and patience made all this possible.

For Judi, who makes it look easy putting up with Bob.

And for Wendy, who inspired every page.

TABLEOFCONTENTS

FOREWORD

RANDYBAUMANN

WEBSTER DEFINES SATIRE as *the use of humor, irony, exaggeration, or ridicule to expose and criticize people's stupidity or vices, particularly in the context of contemporary politics and popular culture.*

But who cares what Webster thinks? What was he, like, three feet tall? And how the hell did he end up living with Alex Karras in the first place? Was he abducted? A poor man's Gary Coleman, if you ask me.

But I digress.

Carbolic Smoke Ball's rise to greatness is a tale as old as time — which, according to Sarah Palin, is only about 6,000 years. And yet, these over-educated, under-sexed Swiftians might never have found their audience if not for the foresight of a brilliant young radio personality named Me.

One day, in an effort to impress a horn-rimmed barista, I pretended to read the *New York Times*, whereupon I spied an article describing the Carbolic Smoke Ball as Pittsburgh's version of The Onion.

A lightbulb went off.

"Why not put them on your hugely popular radio program? Give them the exposure they deserve! And pay them next to nothing! No — pay them NOTHING! You'll sit while they whitewash the fence! And you can bury them in the 9 o'clock hour in case they stink! It's brilliant, I tell you. Brilliant!"

It was then that I realized I was not thinking to myself, but in fact talking rather loudly. The barista was nonplussed.

Since that time, the men of CSB have dedicated themselves to skewering all that finds its way adrift in the mainstream, all the while ignoring the jobs they actually get paid for.

Here's hoping their clients, patients, students, and customers continue to get short shrift.

Randy Baumann co-hosts the great DVE Morning Show on Pittsburgh's top-rated radio station, 102.5 WDVE. He can crow all he wants about not paying us for the radio gig, because we're not paying him for this one.

INTRODUCTION

(But Mostly an Obviously Fawning Love Letter to a
Mysterious, Hilarious, Multifarious Group of Jokesters.)

RICKSEBACK

YOU KNOW WHAT I LOVE? I love the fact that many people see an article from the Carbolic Smoke Ball and don't realize it's a joke.

Carbolic Smoky stuff has long had a sedate and at least semi-serious demeanor on the internet. The simple background. The mostly real news photos. The standard layout. A straightforward journalistic style and ample copy have always given their presentations a look of sobriety and importance. You want to believe them. You just have to be able to read (and have a sense of humor) to see that these articles are jabs and blasts and the best kind of satiric nonsense.

There's no such confusion with a book called *Zombies Ate My Headlines*. A book? Yes. A funny one? Of course. These men (I think they're still all men) who've been destroying Pittsburgh, America, its celebrities, and all of the internet with their deadly wit and spot-on satire have put together this collection of articles and photos that will surely win them new friends who read only printed matter. Old friends of the web-based Carbolic Smoke Ball may want to pick up a copy too, just to see what these guys find book-worthy. And c'mon, you've been getting their wit and world-class intelligence for free for so long, isn't it time you invested a few bucks to help them as they get older?

Since the beginning, people have wondered, *Who are they? Where are they? Why do they do this?* All silly questions. Who cares? As long as they keep pumping out funny stuff.

I don't remember when I first found the web site. You can follow their archives back to July 2005. I'd read their stuff before they first included me (an unsurpassed honor) in an entry in March 2006 — I attacked intrepid *Pittsburgh Post-Gazette* TV critic Rob Owen at a premiere event — but then, of course, I started paying more attention. I put them in my browser's bookmark bar and started quoting their jokes at work. Later that year, there was a mention in the *New York Times,* and the *Post-Gazette*'s Brian O'Neill wrote a column about "One of America's great Web sites," revealing names and occupations of the men who started all this: attorney Tim Murray and banker Bob Haas, along with their henchman Sean Cannon. Then they added missing piece Chad Hermann.

Soon they were Pittsburgh media darlings. They started Friday radio reports on WDVE and fake newspaper work that somehow fit right into the Monday afternoon tabloid edition of the *Pittsburgh Tribune-Review*. They made Pittsburgh a city to respect on the comedy scene. They must have found more collaborators, or they quit their regular jobs or something, because they started chugging out lots of material. And quality stuff.

INTRODUCTION
(cont.)

BY THEN EVERYBODY HAD GOOGLED "carbolic smoke ball" and found out it was some sort of British bogus medical device, a rubber ball with a tube sticking out of it that claimed to protect you from the flu. Its ads promised to pay if the product was ineffective, and somebody called them on it. A landmark legal case resulted. Carlill vs. Carbolic Smoke Ball Company is studied by law students around the world, and the reference is just one of the pointless, goofy quirks that make this comedy troupe so memorable. They also often reference the imaginary Judge Rufus Peckham, who shares a name with a nineteenth century U.S. Supreme Court justice and a face with former Philadelphia mayor Frank Rizzo. I'm not sure what it all means, or if it matters.

All that matters now is that you read the book. And hope that they keep doing what they do. Surely Hollywood is next. Or maybe a Broadway musical. They're some of the world's funniest men, and they deserve our attention.

Let there be no end to the madness.

Rick Sebak is an iconic, award-winning documentary filmmaker for PBS and WQED Multimedia. We love all of his works, but especially "A Hot Dog Program." You know, because we're guys.

CARBOLICSMOKEBALL

presents

ZOMBIES ATE MY NATIONAL NEWS

INVENTOR OF APPLE PIE DEAD AT 86

PITTSBURGH - Noah Swayne was a man of multi-faceted accomplishments, but the one thing he could not do was bake. "It's one of history's great ironies that a man who could not bake is responsible for the quintessential American dessert, apple pie," said President Bush in a statement released shortly after Swayne's death yesterday at 86.

"He loved apples, and he loved pie, and one day it hit him. 'I think I'll combine the two,' he said," explained his widow, Velveeta Lugosi-Swayne. "At first we all thought he had flipped, but he had a vision, and he went for it."

Although best known for the famous dessert, which was referred to as "Swayne Pie" for many years before he insisted it be called by its generic name, Swayne was also responsible for numerous other inventions the world now takes for granted. It was his idea, for example, to make only one side of Scotch Tape sticky. He also invented the extension cord, shirt cardboard, the two-slotted toaster, and the bendy straw. Of all his inventions, the one of which he was most proud is the "Take-a-Penny, Leave-a-Penny" dish, now found in stores around the world. Its official name is the Swayne Dish. Swayne received a royalty on every penny that went into or out of one of the dishes, his widow said.

"Although he refused to talk about it, Noah was also on the team that developed the first atomic bomb," said Mrs. Swayne. "One day, President Harry Truman called the house and said he wanted to name it the Swayne Bomb, but Noah refused. Noah told the President it should be named after the atom itself. 'After all,' Noah chuckled, 'I couldn't have destroyed two Japanese cities without it.'"

Swayne died doing what he loved most: waiting on customers at his hardware store in Brentwood.

"I was at the counter, and Noah opened the cash register, but then he just slumped over," said customer Bob Haas. "With his last ounce of strength, he shut the drawer so I couldn't steal any money."

Swayne's sole request upon his death was that his funeral be conducted at Rodef Shalom Synagogue in Squirrel Hill. "He wasn't a Jew," said his widow, "but he always said it would be neat if everybody thought he was."

POLITICIAN WANTS STATUE OF LIBERTY'S VAGINA REOPENED FOR FIRST TIME SINCE 9/11

NEW YORK - It's time to reopen the Statue of Liberty's vagina to the public, says Rep. Anthony Weiner (D-Forest Hills).

In the aftermath of the September 11 attacks, the National Park Service installed a special heavy-gauge steel chastity device to keep the anatomically correct Lady Liberty from being violated by terrorist projectiles.

"We were very concerned that she might be captured by Islamic Fascists and that the terrorists would have their way with her," explained National Park Service Director Noah Swayne. "One can only imagine the diseases those Mideastern fanatics would have transmitted with their big, ugly missiles."

The chastity belt has never been removed, much to the disappointment of thousands of weekly visitors. Jordan Jones, 17, arrived at Liberty Island yesterday after driving all night from Pittsburgh. He and his five friends, he said, were hoping to take the elevator to "the lady's inner sanctum, dude."

Waiting in line, Jones sneaked a spray of breath freshener and his friends combed their hair, but their hopes were shattered by a park ranger who told them "that part" of the statue is still not open to the public. The boys let fly a string of expletives, then consoled themselves with a visit to the first mammary glands of liberty a little higher up.

Rep. Weiner says it's time to remove the chastity belt. "For generations of red-blooded teenage males, a visit to Lady Liberty's fish factory has been a rite of passage," he explained. "Unlike the terrorists, the only thing infectious about these boys are high jinks and youthful exuberance."

"As long as Lady Liberty's vagina remains closed," Representative Wiener added, "the Islamo-Fascists win, and our young American males lose."

CARBOLICBREAKINGNEWS:

JESSE JACKSON CLAIMS "REFERRING TO HURRICANE VICTIMS AS 'REFUGEES' IS RACIST - JUST ASK ANYONE IN HYMIETOWN"

CHENEY: "ALL CREDIBLE INTELLIGENCE" SUGGESTED HUNTING PARTNER WAS A DUCK, "SO I SHOT HIM"

NASA SHOCKER: LUNAR ROVER LEFT ON MOON IN 1972 IS COVERED WITH PARKING TICKETS!

CAPE CANAVERAL - A satellite photo taken last week reveals that the Lunar Rover, abandoned on the surface of the moon in 1972 by Apollo 17 astronauts, is covered with parking tickets.

NASA Administrator Michael Griffin said he is "very disappointed" that the astronauts apparently left the vehicle, nicknamed the "moon buggy," in a No Parking zone before leaving the moon's surface.

"We need to get someone back to the moon to move that vehicle before it's towed — and to pay those tickets," Griffin explained. "The United States of America will not be known throughout the universe as a parking scofflaw."

MOTHER TERESA AGREES TO ONE HUNDRED THREE MILLION DOLLAR DEAL; NEW CONTRACT WILL MAKE HER THE WORLD'S HIGHEST PAID HUMANITARIAN

CALCUTTA - Mother Teresa has agreed to a new contract that will pay her one hundred three million dollars over the next eight years. The announcement was made this morning at the Missionaries of Charity South Side offices. "This is about being a Member of the Missionaries of Charity for as long as I can be," she said. "I didn't want to go anywhere."

The contract, which includes a twenty-six million dollar signing bonus, makes Mother Theresa the highest paid humanitarian in the world. Dr. Albert Schweitzer, who has devoted his life to improving the health of impoverished Africans, last month signed a ten-year deal worth ninety-five million dollars.

"I'm not going to lie. It was important to my client to be the highest-paid humanitarian in the world," said Bruce Tollner, agent for Mother Teresa. "Now that this is done, Mother can get back to doing what she does best: bringing God's love to millions of downtrodden people dwelling in the bowels of this city."

Mother Teresa expressed her gratitude to the Pope and to her agents. "I'm glad we were able to get this deal done. To be able to finish my career in the city where I started is really special," she said.

POPE BENEDICT CALLS FOR AN END TO POLICE BRUTALITY

OBAMA'S "I HAVE A DREAM SPEECH" MAY HAVE BEEN PLAGIARIZED

SPACE SHUTTLE *ENDEAVOUR* NARROWLY AVOIDS DISASTER AFTER LIFTOFF

REMAINS OF THREE MEN BAKED ALIVE BY PRESIDENT NIXON FINALLY RELEASED TO RELATIVES

FIRST HANDS-TRANSPLANT PATIENT MEETS, SLAPS FACE OF, FIRST FACE-TRANSPLANT PATIENT

WASHINGTON - Tina Sambonia, the world's first hands-transplant patient, met Roberto Montoya, the world's first face-transplant patient, at last night's National Institutes of Health fundraiser.

"We thought it would be a real hoot to have them meet, you know, from a scientific perspective," said Dr. Bradleys Roadhouse, who performed both transplant surgeries.

But the meeting did not go as planned. Unbeknownst to Dr. Roadhouse, the transplanted hands formerly belonged to the wife of the man who donated the face for the

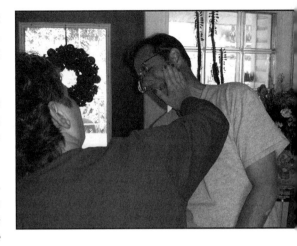

face transplant. That marriage ended unhappily because of the man's indiscretions. When the two transplant patients met last night, the hands-transplant patient involuntarily began slapping the face of the face-transplant patient. Security guards quickly separated the two as the fundraiser's guests watched in stunned silence.

"Through my work with the World Health Organization, I've encountered similar phenomena in Haiti," Dr Roadhouse explained. "To the uninitiated, it can be a little off-putting." Dr. Roadhouse said that as a result of the incident, Mr. Montoya will require additional surgery. "Tina knocked his nose down to his Adam's apple," he chuckled. "I think it's fair to say there hasn't been this much slapping in Washington since the Clintons occupied the White House."

NARCISSISTS PROTEST, WANT SAME-PERSON MARRIAGE LEGALIZED

SAN FRANCISCO -- Thousands of narcissists took to the streets of San Francisco yesterday to protest proposed legislation that would afford same-sex unions all the benefits of traditional marriage. The protesters say the bill isn't fair because it doesn't include same-*person* marriages.

Rally organizer Jingo Bang whipped the crowd into a frenzy: "In the parlance of the civil rights movement," he shouted, "why am I forced to sit in the back of the bus merely because my 'significant other' happens to be *me?*"

The rally was held in the city's Sunset District, the scene of innumerable gay rights rallies where participants traditionally join hands with their partners and sing songs of liberation. But this protest was different, because each protester clasped his own hands and sang a song of his own choosing, creating a disturbing cacophony that drew complaints from as far away as Fisherman's Wharf.

OBAMA / DARK KNIGHT '08

WE'RE WHATEVER YOU NEED US TO BE.

OBAMA TAPS DARK KNIGHT AS VP

GOTHAM CITY, IL - Presumptive Democratic nominee Barack Obama opted for a "sure thing," political insiders say, when he announced the popular film star and blockbuster action hero Batman as his running mate.

"With The Dark Knight's true identity shrouded in secrecy, my political philosophy grounded in myth, and my hubris the stuff of both legend and Greek tragedy, this is surely a ticket of graphic novel proportions," Obama told a cheering Gotham crowd.

Insiders revealed that Sen. Obama also considered former Gotham City District Attorney Harvey Dent as his running mate, but his Vice-Presidential Vetting Team convinced him that adding another Two-Face would not provide sufficient balance for the ticket.

Asked to comment on Senator Obama's choice, presumptive Republican nominee John McCain replied, "Oh, my. Batman and the Joker, together again."

PENNSYLVANIA DEPARTMENT OF TRANSPORTATION SHIPS ORANGE BARRELS TO SAUDI ARABIA TO CURB FUTURE STAMPEDES

Signs to be mounted that read, *"Slow Down - My Daddy Stones Here"*

MINA, SAUDI ARABIA - Only days after a tragic stampede that killed 363 people, Saudi Arabian Interior Spokesman Mansour al Mansour announced that the Saudi government has accepted a bid from the Commonwealth of Pennsylvania's Department of Transportation to improve the orderly flow of pilgrim traffic through the heavily-traveled Al-Jamarat corridor.   "If any organization in the world knows how to slow people down, it's PennDOT," al Mansour said.

The Al-Jamarat corridor has long been known as "the death stretch" by the thousands of pilgrims who stampede through the area during Hajj rush hour. To accomplish the slow-down, PennDOT will place orange barrels in symmetrical positions on both sides of the corridor to "create the illusion that construction is occuring, just like PennDOT does in Pennsylvania," said al Mansour.

PennDOT will also mount a number of signs throughout the corridor to increase safety awareness. One of the signs reads "Slow Down - My Daddy Stones Here." PennDOT officials said work on the Al-Jamarat Corridor project is scheduled to begin in 2020. Completion is scheduled for spring of 2035.

THE 4,000 JEWS WHO FAILED TO SHOW UP FOR WORK AT THE WORLD TRADE CENTER ON SEPTEMBER 11TH ARE SPOTTED AT A MINNESOTA VIKINGS GAME

Arabs wonder, "What are those sneaky Jews up to now?"

CALIFORNIA WILDFIRE SPREADING LIKE ... VERY FAST

CHENEY RELEASES PHOTO PROVING HE DIDN'T SHOOT FELLOW HUNTER; "REAL GUNMAN WAS ON GRASSY KNOLL -- I'M JUST THE PATSY," VICE-PRESIDENT SAYS

PRESIDENT BUSH SENDS BURT REYNOLDS, ADAM SANDLER TO CUBA, WILL BUILD AL-QAEDA PRISON FOOTBALL TEAM TO PLAY AGAINST GUANTANAMO PRISON GUARDS

MEN ON EDGE IN IOWA: HILLARY CLINTON REPORTEDLY HOARDING SHARP INSTRUMENTS, CASTRATION DEVICES

DES MOINES - A town meeting in a local barn last night in Durham, thirty miles south of Des Moines, attracted more than 700 people, all of them men. The subject: reports by local farmers that Sen. Hillary Clinton is canvassing the area, buying up castration devices on the cheap. Men came from five counties to discuss the news, which many of them viewed as "alarming."

Farmer Noah Swayne related a first-person account: "Yesterday morning, two limousines came roaring up the house. Senator Hillary Clinton and her entourage, a bunch of young guys in suits with creamy skin and high pitched, girlish giggles, got out. I answered the door. One of the -- for want of a better word eunuchs -- said to me with kind of a nasty tone, 'Senator Clinton would like to speak with the lady of the house." As he recounted the tale, Swayne wiped sweat from his brow.

"I said, 'Perhaps I can help the Senator?' And this kid says, 'The Senator will not speak with you.' Just like that -- 'the Senator will not speak with you.' OK, I thought, so this is weird. Anyway, I got Ellie, and the Senator smiled at her and shook her hand, and they began chatting away. Now mind you, the Senator never looked at me once the whole time she was there." Swayne had to pause for a drink of water.

"Now here's where it gets completely bizarre. The Senator asked my wife if she had a spare castration device she could sell her."

The men in the audience put their legs together.

Swayne continued: "Well, sir, my wife's eyes opened real wide like she didn't quite make out the words. The Senator repeated herself: 'You wouldn't happen to have a spare castration device you could sell me, would you?' Now my wife was dumbfounded, because that's the last thing she expected to hear from a United States senator. So Ellie said, 'You mean for bulls?' And without missing a beat, the Senator said, 'No, for somewhat smaller mammals.' That's just how she worded it, 'somewhat smaller mammals.'"

Sweat poured from Swayne's forehead, and the room grew completely silent.

"It gets worse. The Senator knew exactly what she wanted," Swayne said. "It either had to be a Burdizzo nine inch or an Emasculator Turbo. She said, 'I find those two work the best.' Well, my wife told her we happened to have a spare Burdizzo we could sell her. So the Senator says, and I quote, 'Would you tell your male to run and fetch it for me?' The whole while she's looking right at my wife, like I wasn't even there. My wife looked at me, like, 'I guess it's alright.' So I went and got it, and my wife **(cont. on p. 17)**

MEN ON EDGE, CLINTON HOARDING EDGES, IN IOWA

(cont. from p. 16) charged her ten dollars or something. The Senator shook her hand."

Swayne took a drink of water. "But here's the part that kept me awake last night: the Senator smiled at her and said, 'I'm buying up as many of these as I can get my hands on, so I'll be ready after I win the election.' And that's an exact quote, because I wrote it down right after she left."

An audible gasp came from the back of the barn. Swayne sat down, wiping his brow. Finally, after a silence that seemed to stretch for a half hour, farmer Ned Newsome rose to his feet and shouted, "I warned you all about that little ballbuster. Now see what we've got here? And with the caucuses right around the corner!"

A clamor arose until Mayor Newt Kiley stood up and raised his hands. "Silence! Now I know how this looks, men, but let's examine the evidence. We have no idea what, or who, Mrs. Clinton intends to use these nasty little devices on, so my advice is that we continue to monitor the situation closely. I suggest we meet here every Tuesday night at 8 o'clock to stay abreast of the latest developments. And no women, please -- we don't know how deep this thing goes." Kiley started to leave, then turned back to the crowd. "And men, you all better get those Obama signs up on your front lawns, like I told you to do months ago."

CLINTON "HOLDS NO BITTERNESS" TOWARD KENNEDY FOR BACKING OBAMA, SNAGS ENDORSEMENT OF SIRHAN SIRHAN

WASHINGTON - Hillary Clinton, saying she "bears no animosity" toward Senator Edward Kennedy for endorsing Barack Obama, today announced that Jordanian immigrant and assassin of Senator Robert Kennedy Sirhan Sirhan has endorsed her.

"Mr. Sirhan is a well-known voice from an historic time in our history," Clinton said in a prepared statement. "Aside from a single, momentary lapse of judgment, he has led a life free of any misconduct, at least any misconduct that the average member of the general public knows about. For that reason, the Clinton campaign embraces his backing."

Later, Clinton was asked if the endorsement was intended as an affront to Sen. Edward Kennedy. "It is what it is," she smirked. She added that Mr. Sirhan pled guilty to the murder of Robert Kennedy only because he knew he could not receive a fair trial in Los Angeles. "Sirhan asked for a change of venue," Mrs. Clinton explained, "but the judge thought he said 'change of menu.' So the judge ordered the prison cafeteria to serve him Chinese."

Analysts say the endorsement could counteract the recent endorsements of Senator Obama by Gennifer Flowers and Paula Jones.

ABU GHRAIB PYRAMID TO HEADLINE NEW LAS VEGAS CIRQUE DU SOLEIL SHOW, "PRISONNIER"

MORE TROUBLE FOR GERMAN SOLDIERS WHO PHOTOGRAPHED THEMSELVES ABUSING CORPSES IN AFGHANISTAN

Woman files suit, claiming: "Hey, that's my skull he's ejaculating on!"

NOBEL-PRIZE-WINNING RUSSIAN AUTHOR ALEXANDER SOLZHENITSYN SIGNS ENDORSEMENT DEAL WITH PFIZER, WILL APPEAR IN NEW VIAGRA ADS

363 KILLED IN STAMPEDE THAT BROKE OUT DURING ANNUAL STONING RITUAL; 512 KILLED IN STONING THAT BROKE OUT DURING ANNUAL STAMPEDING RITUAL

HOMEWORK-EATING DOGS BRED AS PRANK EVOLVE; 160+ IQS ATTRIBUTED TO "SMART DIET"

WASHINGTON - In the mid-1970s, mischievous Georgetown University students selectively bred dogs to produce a homework-eating canine so school children could truthfully tell their teachers "my dog ate it."

The breed, nicknamed "Detention Terrier" for the punishment sometimes meted out to students who fail to do their homework, was widely condemned for its anti-education proclivities.

But thirty years later scientists are astonished to find the breed has evolved into a super sub-species of canine that reads, writes, paints, and composes music. Some of the dogs enjoy a good cigar, and many of them even read *The New Yorker*.

Dr. Jingo Bang, who has written extensively about the dogs, isn't surprised by the breed's rapid evolution. "While other dogs were bred to hunt or to look pretty," Dr. Bang explained, "these little dogs have done nothing but devour vocabulary lists and algebra equations. Is it any wonder they're brilliant?"

MRS. PALSGRAF'S SECOND GRADE CLASS SELECTS ITEMS TO BE INSERTED IN TIME CAPSULE TO BE OPENED IN 2058; FIRST ITEM SELECTED IS MRS. PALSGRAF

PHILADELPHIA - Maryanne Palsgraf, 61, has been known to several generations of second grade students at Spiro T. Agnew Elementary School in Conshohocken, Pennsylvania, as a taskmaster who requires perfection, whether it be coloring within the lines or not tracking snow into her classroom.

"She runs her classroom like it's her own personal fiefdom," said Jeremy Collins, age 7, who asked not to be identified in this story for fear of reprisals.

Yesterday, Mrs. Palsgraf announced that the class would bury a time capsule, not to be opened for fifty years, in the schoolyard. She allowed the class to select the items to insert in the capsule. Without hesitation, the first item the class selected was Mrs. Palsgraf.

"We lured her to the back of the classroom," said Collins, as he colored a space ship attacking another space ship, "and three of my boys clubbed her till she was out cold. Then we called in these tough guys we hired, a couple of eighth graders who've hated Mrs. Palsgraf since back in the day. They cut her up into little pieces, and then we shoved her into the time capsule."

The students plan to tell Mrs. Palsgraf's family about the incident when the time capsule is opened 50 years from now. "We suspect there's some statute of limitations that'll protect us," Collins said. "None of us can read well enough yet to figure that out."

TITANIC SANK FASTER THAN PREVIOUSLY BELIEVED; DIRECTOR JAMES CAMERON ORDERED TO TRIM 15 MINUTES FROM HIS EPIC *TITANIC* TO KEEP IT ACCURATE

FALMOUTH, Mass. - The discovery of two large pieces of *Titanic*'s hull on the ocean floor indicates that the fabled ocean liner sank more quickly than previously believed -- by about 15 minutes, experts revealed on the anniversary of the famous ship's collision with an iceberg.

In light of the revelation, 20th Century Fox has ordered director James Cameron to trim 15 minutes from his 1997 epic *Titanic* to maintain the film's historical accuracy.

An irate Cameron fumed that Fox's tampering with his artistic license is an unwelcome throwback to the days when studio bosses had final say over the director's end-product. "This is just another indication that 20th Century [Fox] is still living in the last century," Cameron said.

COORS LIGHT TRAIN PLOWS THROUGH CROWDED BUILDING; HUNDREDS KILLED, INJURED

NEW YORK - The Coors Light Train, the high-speed means by which refreshing, frost-brewed Coors is magically delivered to the parched throats of grateful consumers, plowed through a crowded mid-town office building yesterday afternoon, killing and maiming hundreds of people. Authorities suspect alcohol was a factor in what the tabloids are calling "The Great Happy Hour Disaster." The conductor reportedly failed a field sobriety test and remains in police custody.

Survivors recalled hearing the faint sounds of a once-popular song by The O'Jays entitled "Love Train" and feeling a stiff, chilly breeze just before the train, known as "The Silver Bullet," hit the building. "It was awful," said David Corbett, a janitor who works the evening shift. "Everywhere I looked there was nothing but bodies and twisted steel. I moved about the survivors, emptying cans of delicious, Rocky-Mountain cold Coors down their throats, but I fear I may have done more harm than good," said Corbett. "I think a couple people may have choked to death."

Coors Chairman Peter Coors issued a statement early this morning expressing his sorrow: "The tears I have shed for the victims and their families are as bitter as the natural Rocky Mountain spring water that we use to brew Coors is pure." Coors promised the full cooperation of everyone in the company with law enforcement and public safety officials as they begin their investigation.

CARBOLIC EXCLUSIVE PHOTO: PARDONED "MOHAMMED TEDDY BEAR TEACHER" GILLIAN GIBBONS CELEBRATES HER FREEDOM WITH HER STUFFED DOG, ALLAH

CAMPAIGN TRAIL MIRACLE: OBAMA TOUCHES LIBERTY BELL, HEALS ITS CRACK

NEW FEDERAL STUDY REVEALS MOST HATE CRIMES DRIVEN BY LOATHING AND DETESTATION

ENHANCED IMAGERY PROVES LOUIS FARRAKHAN BEING HELD HOSTAGE IN *AMERICAN GOTHIC* HOUSE

PRESIDENT DECLARES "WAR ON ERECTILE DYSFUNCTION," SAYS AMERICAN MEN HAVE "INALIENABLE RIGHT TO LIVE FREE AND DIE HARD"

WASHINGTON, D.C. - President Bush asked Congress to authorize funding to wage a war on erectile dysfunction that will abolish the unpleasant, highly-sensitive condition by the year 2012.

"If we can put a man on the moon, we can make sure that every law-abiding, tax-paying male citizen of this great republic is able to use his penis for non-deviant, biblically-approved, monogamous sexual relations with his spouse whenever he wants," said the President.

After the President's address, spokeswoman Dana Perrino hastened to add that the President currently enjoys a robust sexual relationship with the first lady. "The President only became aware of the terrible scourge of erectile dysfunction when he was forced to endure over one-hundred Cialis commercials during last Sunday's NFC Championship game between the Green Bay Packers and New York Giants."

When asked why he chose to make the eradication of this particular male sexual performance issue the thrust of his speech, Ms. Perrino paused before answering. "This is the President's last State of the Union Address," Perrino said. "I think he wants to be remembered as a guy who went out with a bang."

HANS BLIX LOCATES MISSING MATTER IN UNIVERSE

"It's the first thing I've ever actually found," admits former chief UN arms inspector

WASHINGTON, D.C. - Hans Blix, lured out of retirement to help NASA astronomers locate the missing matter in the universe, announced today that he's found most of it. Blix, the former Chief UN Arms Inspector in Iraq who claimed he could find no evidence that Saddam Hussein harbored weapons of mass destruction, said it's the first thing he's ever actually found.

"What I do best is not find things that aren't there," said Blix. "I'm frankly amazed that I was able to find the missing matter -- or anything else, for that matter."

"It was the damnedest thing where we found it," Blix noted. "It was hidden in Baghdad. Isn't that ironic?"

VENUS DE MILO TO GET BREAST ENLARGEMENT TO BOOST CROWDS AT THE LOUVRE

PARIS - For centuries, Venus de Milo, the ancient Greek statute of an armless, naked woman has been considered the epitome of graceful feminine beauty. But the Louvre Museum in Paris, where Venus has been on public display since 1821, is alarmed by the statue's dwindling popularity. Thirty years ago, Venus was the Louvre's most popular attraction. Today, barely a trickle of tourists bother to visit her.

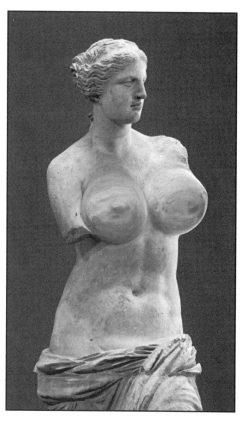

"Let's face it, the real problem is the breasts," said Bob Haas, the first American Director of the Louvre, hired last month after a stint at Euro Disney. "They just don't cut it for modern audiences raised on *Penthouse* -- or so I'm told. Not that I've ever read that publication."

To Haas, the solution is simple. "The way to get the crowds back is through good old-fashioned American breast augmentation," he said. "And I'm not talking about this saline-filled stuff -- you know, where the woman says 'Honey, how do you like my breasts,' and the husband pretends there's a difference but there really isn't, but then he stupidly admits that he *can't* see a difference, which starts a big fight, and he ends up sleeping on the couch for four nights in a row. Not that this ever happened with me and my wife."

Haas wants the largest breasts possible. "I'm talking about string implants, like they use in the adult entertainment industry -- or so I'm told, because how would I know about such things?" he chuckles nervously. "My goal is for this timeless classical beauty to become a testament to men's most wicked desires."

Haas dismisses the criticisms of Parisians who say his plan would crassly eroticize one of the nation's most significant artifacts. "Those are the same snooty Europeans who deride Euro Disney but are first in line to ride the roller coasters," he said. "I will prove to Parisians that I am not crass. I'm going install first-class peep booths with all the amenities so that our male clientele can view Venus properly, with state-of-the-art, coin-operated timer mechanisms that will accept credit cards."

Next year, Haas said he plans to find a sculptor to fit Venus with arms. "Let's face it," he said, "that no-arms look is a real turn-off."

NEWLY RELEASED NIXON TAPE: "I THREW '60 DEBATES TO LET JFK WIN ELECTION BY LOOKING SHIFTY, SWEATY"

On same tape, Nixon pities UN Ambassador George H. W. Bush, for raising "retarded son"

WASHINGTON - Richard Nixon claimed he "threw" the debates with John F. Kennedy leading up to the 1960 election because "Nancy Reagan's astrologer told me the winner would be assassinated in Dallas on November 22, 1963." This is just one of many startling revelations on the newly-released recording of a November 14, 1971, Oval Office meeting between Nixon and Henry Kissinger. Here's an excerpt:

NIXON: . . . It was ten minutes before the first debate, Henry, and Nancy and some tall guy, a real dandy, came tearing into the studio . . .

KISSINGER: Who was the dandy?

NIXON: What's that?

KISSINGER: Who was the dandy?

NIXON: Just . . . [inaudible] . . . Nancy's astrologer. And Nancy's crying about "Dallas" and all this, and "please don't win, Dick," she said. "Let Kennedy win because whoever's elected is going to be gunned down in Dallas on November 22, 1963." That's just what she told me, Henry, she said that very date. Sends chills up my spine in retrospect. Now Henry, I know you may think this is silly, you being a Harvard Jew and all . . .

KISSINGER: No, Mr. President, anything you tell me by its very nature can't be silly.

NIXON: . . . So Nancy, she knows all these Hollywood tricks and so forth. She grabs me and practically dunks my head in this glycerin because -- see Henry, you may not know this, but I don't have any sweat glands. None whatsoever. Nancy said we've got to make it look like I'm sweating like a pig, you know - nervous, so I'd lose the debate. And then she pulled out what they call a stipple sponge and made it look like I had a heavy five o'clock shadow. Truth is, I probably have the lightest beard of any grown man in America.

KISSINGER: The glycerin would have the characteristics of . . .

NIXON: . . . the glycerin would act like sweat, that's right. Then Nancy had this suit of clothes that was a couple sizes too big for me, so it made me look sick, like I'd lost weight or something. Fact is, I couldn't have been more fit. But the most important thing she did was she taught me how I should look around the room like I'm shifty, you know, like can't be trusted. That was the hardest part for me.

KISSINGER: Very clever woman. Too bad she married such a dumbbell.

NIXON: . . . Do you know that when that [*expletive deleted*] Kennedy was shot, I sent Nancy a case of California oranges? **(cont. on p. 27)**

NEWLY RELEASED NIXON TAPE (cont. from p. 26)

KISSINGER: I must say, sir, how fortunate the free world is that you heeded that superstitious advice.

[LATER ON THE SAME TAPE...]

NIXON: . . . in this administration. Bush at the UN has a good future ahead of him.

KISSINGER: But, sir, I am concerned about a man who doesn't like broccoli.

NIXON: Don't be hard on him, Henry. It must be difficult raising a retarded boy in this day and age.

KISSINGER: You mean the older son?

NIXON: Kid's name is George also. Poor young man will never be able to function on his own. Father tells me he thinks everybody -- the butcher, the minister, the crossing guard -- is hiding weapons from him. So sad, Henry. So sad.

AIDES TO TURKEY PARDONED BY PRESIDENT CLAIM "NO SECRET DEAL"

SAN CLEMENTE - The turkey pardoned by President Bush in the annual Thanksgiving ritual thanked the President from his retirement compound in San Clemente and denied rumors of a "secret deal" with Bush.

The turkey and the President never even discussed a pardon, much less cut a deal for one," said the turkey's long-time friend, Bebe Rebozo.

Aides to President Bush explained that Bush had simply become "overwhelmed" with Thanksgiving and decided it was in the national interest to pardon the turkey so the President could get on with the important business of the War on Terror.

The turkey said he plans to spend his time writing his memoirs and acting as an elder statesman on economics, foreign affairs, and poultry issues.

CARBOLICBREAKINGNEWS:

INVENTOR OF HURRICANE CATEGORY SYSTEM FOUND DEAD

Herbert Saffir suffered a heart attack doctors say was a "Five"

ABU GHRAIB ABUSER CONVICTED; HURTS CASE BY BRINGING HER PET TO COURT

PFC England

"Pepe"

BIN LADEN, AL-ZAWAHIRI TO STAR IN HIMALAYAN DINNER THEATER TOUR OF *THE ODD COUPLE*

HOLLYWOOD WRITERS GO ON STRIKE

BUSH TO CALIFORNIA FIRE VICTIMS: "WE WILL HELP YOU REBUILD"

President promises "nice, sub-prime mortgages" for displaced homeowners

BUSH CONSOLES NEW ORLEANS: "I WILL GET THE MAN WHO DID THIS!"

President asks rock 'n roll legend Fats Domino to be "human cork" to plug leak in levee

NEW ORLEANS - Four days after Hurricane Katrina wrought unprecedented devastation on the U.S. Gulf Coast, President Bush arrived to console the jittery Big Easy in the wake of chaos and violence. The President told refugees stranded at the Superdome: "We will hunt down, and we will kill, the evildoers who did this. They can run, but they can't hide."

After visiting the Superdome, the President said he wanted to "survey the destruction" sustained by Harrah's New Orleans casino. The casino sustained only minor damage, but the President was not deterred. Reporters were not permitted to accompany the President on his two-hour visit inside the casino, but a Bush aide was seen exiting the building and then returning with a bag full of quarters.

Before departing the city, the President paid a visit to the home of rock 'n roll legend Fats Domino. Bush implored the 77-year-old pioneer responsible for such classics as "Blueberry Hill" to become a "human cork" to plug up the leak in the levee that had flooded the city. The singer immediately obliged. National Guardsmen helped the singer into a boat, then placed him in the hole where the levee broke.

When asked about the devastation to his home town, Domino said, "Ain't that a shame!"

RAMBO GOES TO CAPITOL HILL, TESTIFIES ON STEROID ABUSE IN ACTION HERO INDUSTRY

WASHINGTON, D.C. - John Rambo, veteran of three Hollywood films and two tours of duty in the Vietnam War, testified before the House Oversight and Government Reform Committee today on the problem of steroids in the action hero industry. Because the Chairman felt his testimony was so important, Congress suspended its standard dress code. Mr. Rambo appeared before the Committee without a shirt, wearing only a bandana and camouflage pants, and spoke for over four hours, his monosyllabic answers delivered in a low, guttural voice that seethed with rage.

The atmosphere inside the hearing room was tense. Representative Elijah Cummings (D-Maryland) scolded the musclebound loner, telling him "the American people have the right to know their action heroes are clean." He went on to condemn what he called the abuse of performance enhancing stimulants by people who defeat entire armies by themselves, using only the weapons they can carry and the wits they've been given by God, while, in the process, sustaining only minor injuries. "Did you see what John McClane did in *Live Free or Die Hard*?" he asked, citing a recent example. He never would have been able to do those things in *Die Hard: With a Vengeance*."

Representative Cummings went on to say he suspects many older, white males looking to prolong the careers in the vigilante business may be tempted to take human growth hormone, or other banned substances. "We have a duty to the integrity of the movies," he said. "We can't let these things happen."

WALT DISNEY COMPANY SECRETLY BUYS UP GAZA STRIP TO BUILD MIDDLE EAST THEME PARK

Mickey Mouse to be named "honorary Jew," circumcised in grand opening extravaganza

Mideast Kingdom
Walt Disney World

Opening in 2009: Donald Duck's Water Torture Ride!

U.S. HOUSE PASSES RESOLUTION CONDEMNING THE ARMENIAN GENOCIDE, THE SPANISH INQUISITION, AND THE CRUSADES; STOPS SHORT OF CONDEMNING CRUCIFIXION

"That was just one guy," said Speaker Nancy Pelosi, "and he was pretty much asking for it."

THE 4,000 JEWS WHO FAILED TO SHOW UP FOR WORK AT THE WORLD TRADE CENTER ON SEPTEMBER 11TH ARE SPOTTED ATTENDING MASS AT THE VATICAN

Arabs wonder, "What are those sneaky Jews up to now?"

OBAMA SUPPORTERS LAUNCH NEW GRASSROOTS EFFORT

*CARBOLIC*BREAKING*NEWS:*

BUSH CLAIMS BELLY LAUGH IN RESPONSE TO QUESTION ABOUT RIOT-RAVAGED FRANCE DUE TO "UNRELATED FUNNY THOUGHT"

VOTERS DEMAND MORE PERSONAL ATTACKS, VEILED RACIAL SLURS IN PRESIDENTIAL CAMPAIGN

HURRICANE CENTER RUNS OUT OF NAMES, RESORTS TO "FORBIDDEN LIST";
FIRST UP: HURRICANE LEE HARVEY OSWALD

"Oswald" builds up steam in Caribbean, heads for Kennedy Compound in Florida

PALM BEACH, FL - For the first time in history, the National Hurricane Center has run out of names for hurricanes, so it must resort to a list of heretofore "forbidden names" that Hurricane Center officials hoped would have to be used. As a result, the next storm in the Atlantic, Hurricane Lee Harvey Oswald, bears the same name as the assassin of President John F. Kennedy.

As of last night, Hurricane Oswald was building up steam in the Caribbean and appeared to be headed straight for Palm Beach Florida, the site of the Kennedy clan's winter compound. Informed of the storm's current trajectory, U.S. Senator Edward M. Kennedy said, "Oh, no, Oswald is coming for us again."

In another irony, the Director of the Hurricane Center, Jack Ruby, bears the same name as the gunman who killed Lee Harvey Oswald two days after President Kennedy's assassination. The current Ruby said he will take all reasonable precautions to keep the citizens of Palm Beach out of harm's way, but Senator Kennedy is skeptical. "Unlike the previous Jack Ruby, let's hope this one takes appropriate action before the harm occurs."

After Hurricane Oswald, according to the National Hurricane Center, will come Hurricane Enron, Hurricane McVeigh, and Hurricane Hitler.

DISCOVERY: THE ROSETTA STONE WAS ROUGH DRAFT

"Every word was so grossly misspelled, it doesn't even resemble English as we know it," study says

LONDON - The Rosetta Stone, the fabled granite slab whose text enabled linguists to decipher hieroglyphs, was merely "a rough draft of someone's incomprehensible musings" and definitely not a final product, a study commissioned by this news source concluded.

"We know it's a rough draft because it's chock-full of misspellings," said former Carbolic Smoke Ball Science Editor, Dr. Jingo Bang, who directed the two-year study at the British Museum where the Rosetta Stone is on permanent display.   Dr. Bang meticulously examined the stone and concluded that "every word is misspelled to the point that it doesn't even resemble English."

The final version of the product has never been found.

ENDEAVOUR LANDING IN JEOPARDY; SHUTTLE CREW MEMBERS FLUMMOXED BY GREMLIN ON THE WING

HOUSTON - The landing of the space shuttle *Endeavour* remains indefinitely postponed pending the resolution of a rare "gremlin on the wing" problem. Crewman Bob Wilson reported the gremlin to his fellow shuttle astronauts shortly after the mission began several weeks ago. His constant screaming was a source of great irritation to his colleagues.

"He kept shouting. 'There's a man on the wing!' over and over again," said astronaut Patricia Matheson. "We thought he was having a reaction to some bad Tang."

After several days, the gremlin revealed himself to the entire crew, standing on the wing and holding a sign telling them to "GO TO HELL." He hasn't moved since.

Commander Dominic Gorie said liability issues surrounding the probable incineration of the gremlin upon *Endeavour*'s re-entry to Earth's atmosphere have forced him to keep the shuttle aloft. "We just don't have the kind of funding these days that a protracted wrongful death lawsuit with the gremlin's family would cost," said Commander Gorie. "It's more important for us to spend our limited resources in space instead of the courts."

Commander Gorie said he had no idea how the gremlin ended up on the shuttle wing. "We did a thorough sweep of the shuttle for stowaways, monsters, aliens, and gremlins before lift-off. The only thing I can think of is that somebody on the inspection crew must have done a half-assed job."

CARBOLICBREAKINGNEWS:

MIT STUDY SHOWS THAT HEAT, AT ADEQUATE TEMPERATURES, CAN PREVENT FREEZING

BIGFOOT ON ICE TURNS OUT TO BE A HOAX; EXAMINATION OF THE CARCASS REVEALS IT'S ACTUALLY JANET RENO

OBAMA VOWS TO CREATE NEW CABINET POSITION: SECRETARY OF RENOUNCEMENTS

RESIDENTS OF NEIGHBORHOOD OF MAKE-BELIEVE ON EDGE AFTER RASH OF DRIVE-BY SHOOTINGS, ASSAULTS

MAKE BELIEVE - King Friday XIII, benevolent monarch who has ruled the Neighborhood of Make Believe for nearly forty years, will hold a news conference this morning to announce the formation of a gang task force to combat a series of random acts of violence in his kingdom.

Lady Elaine Fairchild, sole curator of the Museum-Go-Round, a popular tourist destination known for its world-famous Hall of Boomerangs, said her place has been shot up twice in the past week. "It's been hell sleeping at night, toots," said Ms. Fairchild. "I hope Friday can get this thing under control."

Daniel Striped Tiger, who retired to the Neighborhood after spending twenty years working for Siegfried and Roy, said he's noticed a change. "I grew up in this place. I never worried about getting stabbed or pistol-whipped when I was a cub." Daniel said things began to change when King Friday decided to tear down Corn Flake S. Pecially's Factory and build a casino. "That place just attracts the wrong element," he said.

Last evening, Ms. Henrietta Pussycat was assaulted while returning home from a visit with Dr. Bill Platypus. The suspect, described as a tall white male wearing a cardigan sweater and sneakers, remains at large. A spokesman for the King said his royal highness declined to blame gamblers for the spike in crime but vowed to restore law and order.

POPE BENEDICT SUSPECT IN RASH OF WASHINGTON D.C. ROBBERIES; GIANT "KEY TO CITY" USED TO ACCESS HOMES, BANK VAULTS

WASHINGTON - Washington D.C. Mayor Adrian Fenty has issued a plea to Pope Benedict XVI to turn himself in to police tonight after authorities issued a warrant for his arrest in connection with a series of burglaries in the Washington D.C. metropolitan area. Since Tuesday, numerous civic and financial institutions have suffered incalculable losses in a string of after-hours break-ins. No signs of forced entry were apparent to investigators, leading police to conclude that the perpetrator must have access to each of the buildings.

Mayor Fenty, who presented the Pope with a key to the city during a ceremony last Tuesday, was clearly upset. "When I gave the key to His Holiness, I asked him to be careful about who he gave it to. I want to remind all of you that the Pope has not been charged with a crime. I'm sure there is a very simple explanation for how so much money, art, jewels, and cars could have been stolen in such a short period of time and with such relative ease, and I'm certain that explanation does not implicate the Pontiff or his recently obtained key that opens every lock from Arlington to Bethesda."

EMOTIONAL JOURNALISTS MOURN TIM RUSSERT, APPLY FOR HIS JOB

WASHINGTON, DC - Journalists from around the nation converged on the nation's capital yesterday to attend a memorial service for "Meet the Press" host Tim Russert, and then to apply for his job.

"We have lost a valued colleague and role model whose legacy of fairness and tenacity are irreplaceable," said one newsman, wiping tears from his face during the gathering at Kennedy Center. "Do you think they'd start me at what he was making?"

The grief hit especially hard at out-of-town newsmen from medium market stations. Les Williams, anchor at WJLJ in Bismarck, N.D., said he spoke for many when he said Russert was viewed as a guiding figure on which to model countless careers.

"He had this direct lighting about him. It hid his double chin and made his hair look fuller. We don't have the crew for that sort of thing in Bismarck. God, I hope they're at least going to look at my audition tapes," Williams said, pocketing a dozen funeral cards to impress his children and colleagues back home.

A cortege more than a mile long followed Russert's casket to a suburban Washington cemetery where his old pastor, the Rev. Conor Fitzwilliams, offered a prayer. Commending Russert's soul to God, the Rev. Fitzwilliams urged mourners to "remember the Tim we knew so well, but more importantly, to honor that memory by carrying on his tradition. I know I'm going to try to do that. And if the President of NBC News is here, I'd like a word with him after we're finished."

CARBOLIC*BREAKING*NEWS:

PRESIDENT BUSH MAKES SHORT SHRIFT OF CRITICS' CONCERNS OVER IRAQ WAR, PROMISES TO MAKE LENGTHY SHRIFT OF THEM FROM NOW ON

CASPAR WEINBERGER'S GHOST SPOTTED AT WHITE HOUSE; STAFFERS SAY IT "SEEMS FRIENDLY"

DEBUTING TONIGHT ON IRAQI TV: "THE SUNNI & SHIA COMEDY HOUR"

CHIEF JUSTICE REHNQUIST DIES;
HIGH COURT DIVIDED 4-4 ON CAUSE OF DEATH

Justice Scalia issues stinging dissent, finds "no textually demonstrable support"
in the plain words of the constitution for cause of Chief Justice's death

CIVIL RIGHTS MOVEMENT BEGAN WITH TRANSCRIPTION ERROR

In 1962, singer and activist Joan Baez invited Dr. Martin Luther King Jr. and his wife to dinner. When Dr. King telephoned Baez to accept, he told her secretary, "Tell Joan we shall come over," but the secretary erroneously scribbled, "Tell Joan we shall overcome."

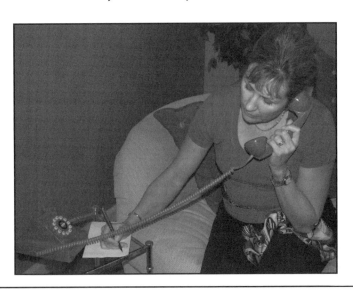

BAGHDAD WEATHERMAN SLAIN BY SHIITE MILITIA AFTER DELIVERING FORECAST OF "PARTLY TO MOSTLY SUNNI"

BAGHDAD *Super Severe Weather Center Forecast.*

Monday, August 18th

High: 108   Low: 89

Partly to Mostly Sunni

40% Chance of Suicide Bombings

Now with Extra Norad Doppler Green Zone Team Coverage!

VICE-PRESIDENT CHENEY SURVIVES OFFICE FIRE, DECLARES, "ONLY SILVER BULLETS CAN KILL ME"

BIN LADEN, AL-ZAWAHIRI AT ODDS OVER SPRING CLEANING; AL QAEDA CHIEF SAYS PEOPLE LEADING JIHAD "DO NOT SCRUB CAVES"

PESHAWAR - Osama Bin Laden, the world's most hunted terrorist and self-proclaimed leader of a global holy war against America, refuses to participate in traditional spring cleaning rituals. Bin Laden announced his intentions in a video released to the Al-Jazeera network.

"My roommate, Dr. Al-Zawahiri, has pestered me for weeks about giving this cave a good scrubbing, but I'm sick of looking at these rock walls," he said. "Let him take me out once in a while, and I'd be more agreeable to performing domestic chores."

Bin Laden went on to describe a litany of insults to which he has been subjected by Dr. Al-Zawahiri since the two men went into hiding following the US invasion of Afghanistan in 2001. Chief among them was a failure of Dr. Al-Zawahiri to express gratitude to Mr. Bin Laden for his willingness to prepare food on a daily basis.

"Not a day goes by that he doesn't come home from a hard day of fomenting hatred and not find a hot meal on the table," Bin Laden complained. "You think he'd ever say thanks?"

CIA officials who examined the tape believe it is authentic. One analyst, speaking on condition of anonymity, said "the walls of that cave appear to have built up a significant amount of grime and dust," leading the agency to conclude it was made within the past several weeks.

JESSE JACKSON WORRIED BARACK OBAMA WILL DISPLACE HIM AS HEAD BLACK

HOUSTON - Jesse Jackson has confided in friends that he hopes Barack Obama loses the Democratic nomination to Hillary Clinton because he fears Obama is displacing him as head black.

To heal the rift, Sen. Obama has reportedly reached out to Rev. Jackson and promised that if elected, he will put Jackson in charge of accepting all apologies from racists, a job Jackson has performed informally for several years. A well-placed campaign source said that plans to create a cabinet-level position for Jackson called Secretary of Racial Apologies. Jackson reportedly is eager to discuss the position with Obama and has sent him a note inviting him to dinner next week in "Hymietown."

CARBOLIC FLASHBACK: APRIL 4, 1938: "HI-DE-HO MEETS HEIL-DE-HO! CAB CALLOWAY, HITLER DISCUSS FUTURE OF NATIONAL SOCIALISM, JIVE"

BERLIN - Popular American bandleader Cab Calloway met with German leader Adolf Hitler yesterday in an attempt to improve relations between their two countries. "The Fuehrer is a righteous cat. He may be from Bavaria, but he's from southern Bavaria, if you dig what I'm putting down," said Mr. Calloway, as both men emerged from the conference room. "I haven't felt this good since Minnie the Moocher's wedding day."

Mr. Calloway described his discussions with Mr. Hitler as "solid" and "jive-free." According to a copy of the minutes released to the press, topics included ways to alleviate tensions between Germany and Czechoslovakia and the possibility of bringing National Socialism to Harlem. Mr. Calloway declined to address specific details, but hinted that a solution to the Czech crisis is imminent. "The Fuehrer is hep to the idea of peace in our time, you dig? My man Adolf knows that war ain't nothin' but a solid drag."

Mr. Calloway addressed the Reichstag last night. After a rousing introduction by Dr. Josef Goebbels, Mr. Calloway walked to the podium as a great, thunderous chant of "Heil De Heil De Heil De Ho" filled the chamber. A clearly moved Calloway wiped his eyes and managed to mutter "Thanks, Daddy," before stepping aside to regain his composure. His remarks were interrupted by applause numerous times.

Following a weekend at Mr. Hitler's Berchtesgaden home, Mr. Calloway flies to Rome for a three-day visit with Italian strongman Benito Mussolini.

CARBOLIC*BREAKING*NEWS:

PAKISTAN PRESIDENT MUSHARRAF DENIES BIN LADEN HAS SAFE HARBOR IN PAKISTAN

And to suggest he's hiding in my country -- or on the third floor of my presidential palace in the corner suite facing East -- is just ridiculous," he said

POLLS SHOW SUPPORT BUILDING TO BUY OUT REMAINING MONTHS OF PRESIDENT BUSH'S CONTRACT

CARBOLIC EXCLUSIVE: FIRST LOOK AT NEXT WEEK'S *NEW YORKER* COVER

Magazine's editor relents, apologizes, promises to change

NEW YORK, NY - In a surprising reversal, the editor of *The New Yorker* admitted today he made a "serious error in judgment" by running this week's controversial cover illustration of Senator Barack Obama and his wife dressed as Islamic terrorists.

Editor-in-Chief David Remnick issued a statement saying that he and his staff have "learned much" from the experience, and that they promise "never to make the same mistake again."

"We apologize to Senator Obama, to his wife Michelle, and to his supporters for our reckless, tasteless, and offensive cover art," Remnick wrote. "After consulting with the editors of many of our peer publications, as well as with members of Senator Obama's staff, we now see and fully appreciate the error of our ways. From now on, our cover illustrations will afford Senator Obama the same reverence and appreciation he receives from every other magazine in America."

Remnick added that he hopes this week's cover, which he called "a new testament to our good faith," will "set the record straight" and "show America the real Barack Obama."

96-YEAR-OLD WOMAN DIES; "CURSE OF TITANIC" CLAIMS ANOTHER VICTIM

LONDON - Barbara West Dainton, believed to be one of the last two survivors from the sinking of the *Titanic* in 1912, has died in England at age 96. The last American survivor, Lillian Gertrud Asplund, died in Massachusetts last year at age 99.

Sir Osmond Swayne, *Titanic* historian, explained that the deaths of Ms. Dainton and Ms. Asplund within a year of each other are an "astounding" coincidence. "What are the odds that two women in their late 90s would just happen to die in the same year? And doesn't it strike you as an incredible contrivance that they both supposedly died of 'natural causes' connected with old age? Or that they both just happened to live in nursing homes, even though they were separated by the whole Atlantic Ocean? No, this is more than coincidence. There's only one possible explanation: the curse of the *Titanic*," he explained.

Sir Osmond explained that the "Curse of the *Titanic*" has been taking lives since 1912. "The curse actually started with the sinking, because many lives were lost that night."

"Do you know what this means?" he asked. "No one who was on that boat that night is safe."

IRANIAN PRESIDENT LEARNS LARRY KING IS A JEW, MURDERS HIM ON THE AIR

NEW YORK - Iranian President Mahmoud Ahmadinejad, visiting New York to address the U.N. General Assembly, murdered CNN talk icon Larry King last night during an exclusive appearance on "Larry King Live."

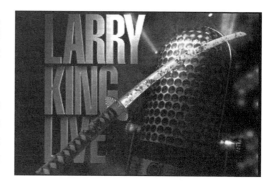

The incident occurred about halfway through the interview, when Mr. King asked Mr. Ahmadinejad if he thought President Bush was a "schmuck." The Iranian president's eyes glared suddenly, and he sprang from his chair.

"Are you a Jew, Larry?" he challenged Mr. King in perfect English. "Tell me the truth: are you a Jew?" Middle East experts later said that Mr. King's use of the word "schmuck" triggered Mr. Ahmadinejad's reaction. Mr. King's eyes widened, his hands trembled, and his face turned white. "I was born a Jew," Mr. King meekly replied.

Mr. Ahmadinejad whipped out a saber he had concealed in his pants and quickly slit Mr. King's throat. Mr. King slumped to the floor and let out a death gurgle. Blood spewed from his throat.

Security guards charged the set. "Diplomatic immunity!" Mr. Ahmadinejad cried, raising his hands in the air. "Diplomatic immunity!"

Mr. King was rushed to Mount Sinai Hospital, where he was pronounced dead. Mr. Ahmadinejad was questioned by New York police and released, due to diplomatic immunity.

CNN announced that "Larry King Live" will be renamed "Larry King Dead," and that tomorrow night's annual tribute to Mickey Rooney, with guests Elizabeth Taylor and Debbie Reynolds, would be guest-hosted by Charles Grodin.

CARBOLICBREAKINGNEWS:

"BIG BANG" MACHINE SHUT DOWN; NEIGHBORS COMPLAIN ABOUT NOISE, CREATION OF ALTERNATE UNIVERSE

RAUL CASTRO TAPS DESI ARNAZ JR. AS NEW VP

CINDY McCAIN VISITS GEORGIAN REFUGEES, OFFERS THEM JOBS CLEANING HER HOMES

JEWS SHOW DISPLEASURE OVER MEL GIBSON'S ANTI-SEMITIC TIRADE BY RETURNING THEIR COPIES OF *THE PASSION OF THE CHRIST*

IDENTITY SHOCKER: JIMMY CARTER AND ELEANOR ROOSEVELT ARE THE SAME PERSON!

ELEANOR ROOSEVELT, 1918   JIMMY CARTER, 2008

McCAIN PICKS PALIN

Choice already sparking controversy, as rumors
swirl that nominee may not be a U.S. citizen

NBC NAMES MICHAEL PHELPS NEW HOST OF "MEET THE PRESS"

"We love his focus and his intensity," said NBC News President Steve Capus.
"And after our Olympic Coverage, we figured the transition would be indistinguishable."

POPEYE DEAD; BELOVED SAILOR MAN SUCCUMBS TO *E COLI* AFTER CONSUMING BAGGED SPINACH

KING SYNDICATE TOWN - Beloved animated mariner Popeye the Sailor Man died of massive kidney failure yesterday after consuming a bag of raw spinach. It is believed the triple-washed, cello-packed spinach was infected with the E Coli bacteria.

Authorities have traced the bag to Natural Selection Foods, a company based in San Juan Bautista, California. Natural Selection Foods is owned by Bluto, a man known for his violent altercations with Popeye over the affections of the anorexic, oval-eyed Olive Oyl. Mr. Bluto issued a statement this morning disavowing any knowledge that the spinach he presented Popeye in the middle of yesterday's brawl was filled with anything but "green leafy goodness." He added that his thoughts and prayers were with Popeye and his family, and that he looked forward to ravaging Ms. Oyl now that his former romantic rival was enduring the eternal flames of perdition. He concluded his statement with a deep, dark, drawn-out laugh.

According to Ms. Oyl, Popeye staggered into his house and up the stairs early Sunday morning after a long night of brawling. He collapsed as he entered his bedroom and fell into Ms. Oyl's arms. "It looks like I'm finished. I ate tainted spinach. Tell Bluto I hate his guts," he said. "Then he gave two mournful blows of his corncob pipe, and died," Ms. Oyl said.

Lawyers for Ms. Oyl were simultaneously seeking a restraining order and preparing a wrongful death suit against Mr. Bluto. Criminal charges may still be filed. Funeral arrangements were incomplete.

NASA BREAKS NEWS TO SPACE SHUTTLE TEACHER THAT *ENDEAVOUR* HAS POTENTIALLY SERIOUS GASH, TAKES BETS ON HER REACTION

CAPE CANAVERAL - NASA finally broke the news to space shuttle *Endeavour*'s most famous astronaut, school teacher Barbara Morgan, that the spacecraft's thermal shield has a potentially serious gash.

"Nobody wanted to tell her," chuckled NASA Administrator Michael Griffin. "I guess we thought she'd give us detention or something," he said, barely able to contain himself.

NASA feared alarming Ms. Morgan because of the uncanny similarity of the problem to the one that doomed the shuttle *Columbia* in 1986. But Griffin ultimately decided Morgan had to be told.

"We had an office pool as to how the teacher would take it," Mr. Griffin said, smiling. "Now I have to tell you, I never win anything, but damn if I didn't bet twenty dollars that she would throw her lunch tray at the wall -- and that's exactly what she did. So, yes, it was a good payday for me."

ATOMIC SCIENTISTS DISCOVER BATTERIES DEAD IN DOOMSDAY CLOCK, HAVE "NO IDEA" HOW CLOSE WORLD IS TO ANNIHILATION

CHICAGO - The atomic scientists at the University of Chicago who maintain the Doomsday Clock, the timekeeper that warns of possible global annihilation, discovered today that the clock's batteries have been dead for an indeterminate amount of time. Records indicate the batteries were last known to be functional in 2002, and that the clock's big hand has been at seven minutes before midnight since then. Midnight represents the end of the world.

With the dead batteries, scientists say they have 'no idea' how close the world really is to total destruction. "For all we know, we could be just seconds away," said a grim Dr. Noah Swayne, director of the Bulletin of Atomic Scientists that maintains the clock.

JOHN McCAIN ARRESTED FOR BREAKING AND ENTERING; SENATOR CLAIMS INNOCENT MISTAKE: "I DON'T KNOW WHICH HOUSES ARE MINE"

WASHINGTON, DC - Senator John McCain was arrested last night and charged with breaking and entering after a woman found him sprawled out naked and asleep on a bed in her Georgetown home.

It was the third time this month that McCain has been booked for breaking-and-entering-related charges after being discovered inside someone else's home.

McCain's defense in each case has been the same: he doesn't know how many houses he and his wife, Cindy, own. "I must have guessed wrong again," said McCain.

CARBOLICBREAKINGNEWS:

CATHOLIC SCHOOLS TO END SEGREGATION OF CLASSES BY GENDER, WILL NOW SEGREGATE BY "THE SAVED AND "THE DAMNED"

17 MASSACHUSETTS HIGH SCHOOL GIRLS ENTER INTO "PREGNANCY PACT"

172 Massachusetts high school boys get wind of plan, sign up to assist

POPE LISTED AS "DOUBTFUL" FOR ASH WEDNESDAY; HIGH ANKLE SPRAIN COULD SIDELINE PONTIFF FOR ENTIRE LENTEN SEASON

VATICAN CITY - The Vatican issued a press release yesterday listing Pope Benedict XVI as "doubtful" for today's Ash Wednesday services. According to front office sources, the Pope sustained a high ankle sprain while distributing communion during Mass last Sunday.

Witnesses in the communion line said it appeared the Pope was in severe pain as he was helped from the altar by several concelebrants and Church trainers. He was transported through the sacristy on a cart. An MRI performed shortly thereafter revealed the nature of the injury.

The Holy Father was seen by reporters walking around Vatican offices the past several days wearing a boot-cast. He waved off members of the media who pressed him for comment.

Because a high-ankle sprain can take between eight and ten weeks to heal, the Pope's status for the upcoming Lenten season would appear to be in jeopardy. An anonymous source within the Holy See said, "we're hopeful he'll be back by Pentecost, but it's likely he'll be out at least until the Ascension."

If Benedict XVI is unable to go next Wednesday, the task of leading the faithful would fall to the second-string, or back-up, Pope. A back-up Pope hasn't been called upon since the 1303-1304 Lenten season, when the league had a branch office in Avignon, France.

GIDEONS BREAK INTO HOTELS, TAKE BACK BIBLES

NEW YORK - In an unprecedented rash of orchestrated burglaries, several hundred members of the Gideons International broke into hotel rooms across America last night to take back the Bibles their organization donated.

"People aren't reading them, and we want them back. It's that simple," said a member of the Gideons who spoke on condition of anonymity. "The Lord giveth, and he taketh away. So do the Gideons."

Hotel managers called the burglaries atypical. "It was the most polite break-in I've ever seen," said Bradleys Roadhouse, manager of the Waldorf-Astoria. "They took back the Bibles, but they also turned down the beds and put chocolates on the pillows."

BERT AND ERNIE, LONG-TIME COMPANIONS JOINED IN CIVIL UNION, WILL RUN BED AND BREAKFAST IN VERMONT

BENNINGTON - Bert and Ernie, the comic duo who made each visit to Sesame Street a laugh-filled trip for millions of pre-school children, were joined in a civil union at City Hall yesterday. The newlyweds plan to open a bed-and-breakfast resort in the Green Mountains. The ceremony was performed by Thad Gould, the Chief Justice of the Vermont Supreme Court.

"This has been a long-time coming," said Chief Justice Gould. "Bert, I'm glad you finally decided to make an honest man out of Ernie."

The steps of City Hall were packed with well-wishers and activists seeking to capitalize on the celebrity of the individuals involved to advance their own agendas. "Bert and Ernie were forced to keep their true feelings bottled up inside a dingy, below-street flat for over thirty years," shouted one man. "Poor Ernie spent a lifetime professing his love for a rubber ducky, because that's what society made him do!"

Numerous friends from the old Sesame Street neighborhood attended the ceremony. Oscar the Grouch, who has been an outspoken opponent of human feelings, was clearly unhappy. "What a waste of time. This whole thing stinks worse than the bottom of my garbage can." Mr. Grouch was pessimistic about the long-term prospects of the newly-legalized relationship. "Believe me, Ernie is really driving Bert crazy. Bert only agreed to this to shut Ernie up. It won't be long before the cops find Ernie on the floor with Bert's paper clip collection shoved down his throat."

TIME MACHINE INVENTOR WANTS TO RETURN TO *TITANIC*, SAVE "MEN AND CHILDREN FIRST"

PHILADELPHIA - To commemorate the anniversary of the April 15, 1912 sinking of *Titanic*, time-machine inventor Dr. Chad Hermann has issued a call to feminist scholars and Women's Studies professors to return to the ship's deck on that fateful night and help him reverse the sexism practiced by men who insisted on saving "women and children first." Thus far, no one has accepted the offer.

One professor, who asked to remain anonymous, explained, "I'm for equality and all that, but he's nuts."

*CARBOLIC*BREAKINGNEWS:

SPECIAL PROSECUTOR SAYS KARL ROVE MAY HAVE OUTED ELLEN DeGENERES

TODAY'S POLITICAL CARTOON FROM THE *TEHRAN POST-GAZETTE* ENTITLED, "MOHAMMED SCOWLS AT THE WEST"

IN LIGHT OF INDICTMENT AGAINST HIM, PLANET XENON WILL NO LONGER RETAIN DR. CYRIL WECHT FOR ALIEN AUTOPSIES

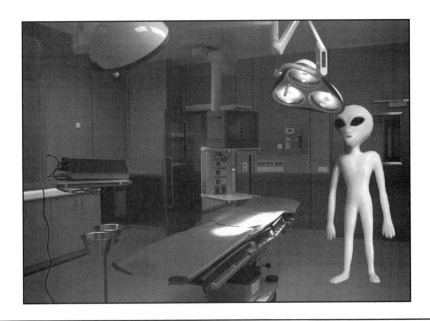

SOUTHWEST AIRLINES PILOT IN MIDWAY CRASH PEEVED AT PASSENGERS FOR "ACTING ALL UPSET" ABOUT LANDING

"Up until the crash on the runway, the flight was a load of laughs," pilot says

JESSE JACKSON: INNER CITY'S "BIGGEST PROBLEM" IS BLACK-ON-BLACK HORN HONKING

AFTER DENOUNCING AS "IDIOTS" PEOPLE WHO BELIEVE IN THE IDEA OF A LIVING CONSTITUTION, JUSTICE ANTONIN SCALIA IS BRUTALLY ATTACKED BY HIS COPY OF THE DOCUMENT

WASHINGTON, DC - Hours after Supreme Court Justice Antonin Scalia denounced as "idiots" those who believe in a "living Constitution" that changes akin to a living organism, Scalia claims that his own copy of the Constitution brutally attacked him, and that he narrowly escaped with his life. One of Scailia's law clerks said the Justice is badly bruised and hysterical in a Washington, D.C. hospital, but is expected to make a full recovery.

The alleged attack occurred last night after Scalia spoke at a Federalist Society dinner where he rejected the "living Constitution" concept. Scalia returned to his chambers at the Supreme Court Building at approximately 10:30 to pick up some papers. He claims he turned on the lights and then heard the sound of breaking glass in the credenza where he keeps his yellowed, dog-eared copy of the Constitution. According to Scalia, the Constitution stood up on its own and, without warning, leaped toward his face and knocked him to the floor.

The document proceeded to maul him, the Justice said, leaving him with multiple paper cuts about the neck and face. Scalia was able to grab a paper shredder next to his desk, causing the Constitution to dart instinctively behind a curtain. Scalia then ran out of the building and sought medical attention.

Police confiscated the purported "living Constitution," which showed no signs of having been animated, from Scalia's chambers. Although investigators initially discounted Scalia's account as "fantastic," testing today revealed that inkprints on the Justice's throat are the same as those belong to the document.

FDA RECALLS "RAID" INSECTICIDE BECAUSE OF HIGH INCIDENCE OF LIFE-THREATENING DISEASE IN INSECTS

WASHINGTON, DC - The Food and Drug Administration ordered all lots of popular insecticide Raid pulled from store shelves this morning following the results of studies showing that Raid poses an "alarmingly" high incidence of life threatening disease to ants and flying insects.

SEMEN FOUND TO BE "PERFECT RAW MATERIAL" TO PRODUCE BIODIESEL

Ejaculate expected to displace oil to fuel cars by 2010; teen males to be the new Sheiks

WASHINGTON, DC - Feminist writers who have provocatively pondered whether men still serve a useful purpose since women can do everything men can do and can even reproduce without a mate are about to get an answer they may not like, and from an unlikely source.

The Congressional Commission on Alternative Fuels yesterday released a comprehensive report that shows semen is the "most efficient, most cost-effective -- in short, the perfect" -- raw material to produce biodiesel fuel.

Given the potential supply of ejaculate capable of being produced by American males," the report concludes, "by 2010, semen likely will replace oil to power virtually every American motor vehicle."

The development could produce a sea change for American males, the report explains. For some, the news is a godsend: "A mother who suspiciously asks her son what he's up to alone in his room might be pleasantly surprised when he tells her that he's doing his part to reduce American dependency on the stranglehold of foreign oil," the report explains.

It could also have wide-ranging repercussions that will require more careful study, the report cautions. Teenage males likely will become the new Sheiks, owners of a seemingly endless supply of fuel," the report explains. "It is conceivable they will control most of the world's wealth." The report concludes: "Somewhere there's a skinny boy with nerdy glasses who's going to be wealthier than Bill Gates."

Kim Gandy, President of NOW, is urging all women to continue using dirty, fossil-fuel based products instead of semen, regardless of the cost or the harm to America, "for obvious reasons."

CARBOLICBREAKINGNEWS:

ABU DHABI BECOMES MAJOR CITIGROUP INVESTOR; CITIGROUP CHAIRMAN FRED FLINTSTONE EXCLAIMS, "ABU DHABI DOO!"

SALVATION ARMY, KNIGHTS OF COLUMBUS DEPLOYED TO IRAQ

JERRY LEWIS STILL DOING TELETHON BECAUSE NO ONE HAS THE HEART TO TELL HIM MUSCULAR DYSTROPHY WAS CURED 15 YEARS AGO

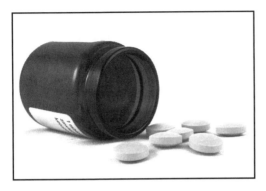

LAS VEGAS - Comic legend Jerry Lewis joined friends and entertainers this Labor Day weekend for his 42nd annual Telethon, supposedly to benefit the Muscular Dystrophy Association. While the whole world knows muscular dystrophy was cured fifteen years ago, Lewis trudges on year after year, oblivious to the news. "I'll never wave the white flag in the fight against muscular dystrophy so long as it still exists," Lewis said yesterday.

Lewis thinks the telethon raises tens of millions of dollars annually. In fact, the pledges are all made up. There is no Muscular Dystrophy Association, and no one is searching for a cure. "There's no need for any of that any more," said telethon sidekick Ed McMahon. "But Jerry thinks there is."

"We tried to tell him [about the cure] when it happened back in '92, but it just didn't sink in," explained McMahon. "I kept repeating it over and over, shaking him by the shoulders, but all I got was a blank stare. We decided never to bring it up again, because we figured it would kill him." McMahon shakes his head sadly. "This entire telethon is a charade to keep a wonderful man happy. In his mind, he's helping a lot of people."

TEN-YEAR-OLD FLOOD AND MD VICTIM ACCUSED OF "TELETHON DOUBLE-DIPPING" FROM JERRY LEWIS & KATRINA FUNDRAISERS

Jerry Lewis: "I'm ashamed that Joey is crippled."

NEW ORLEANS - When ten-year old muscular dystrophy victim Joey Smith was stranded with thousands of other New Orleans refugees in the Superdome last week in the wake of Hurricane Katrina, his wheelchair-bound condition elicited an outpouring of nationwide sympathy. But sympathy turned to outrage when Jerry Lewis accused Smith of "telethon double-dipping" by accepting substantial donations and lavish gifts from both Lewis' MDA organization and the Hurricane Katrina fundraiser.

"He's capitalizing on his condition to be 'made whole' twice. There's a word for people like Joey, and it' 'thief,'" said Lewis. Lewis added that Smith needs to make up his mind, "does Joey want to be one of 'Jerry's Kids' or does he want to be one of the so-called hurricane victims who didn't have the sense to come in out of the rain? If it's the latter, I'll buy Joey a f - - - ing umbrella."

Smith, contacted on his new yacht somewhere in the Caribbean, said Lewis is just a "cranky old man with too much time on his hands. "Can I help it if the fat [expletive] is still mad that Dean dumped him?"

OBAMA DISTANCES HIMSELF FROM YET ANOTHER SUPPORTER, BRINGING TOTAL TO 4,092

CHICAGO - Democratic presidential candidate Barack Obama said Thursday he is "deeply disappointed" by supporter Rev. Michael Pfleger's remarks that mocked Hillary Rodham Clinton. Pfleger is the 4,092nd person from whom Obama has distanced himself in the past month, starting with the Reverend Jeremiah Wright and including Obama's wife, Michelle.

"I was going to say that Father Pfleger's divisive, backward-looking rhetoric doesn't reflect the country I see," Obama said in what supporters dubbed a landmark speech on distancing oneself from racism and its practitioners. "I was going to say that Father Pfleger is like a crazy old uncle who says things I don't agree with. But the fact is, how many crazy old uncles can a person have? Reverend Wright was like a crazy old uncle; my wife was like a crazy old uncle. If I'm to be believed, I've got thousands of crazy old uncles. I mean, let's get real -- nobody has that many uncles.

"Maybe the comments of these nutty people really do reflect the country we live in, and I'm just too blind to see it," he said. "I'm starting to wonder, maybe it's me."

Asked if this meant he would decline the nomination or drop out of the race, Obama replied, "Hell no. I beat that [expletive] fair and square, and I'm gonna beat that old [expletive] too. I'm still the man!"

CARBOLICBREAKINGNEWS:

PRESIDENT BUSH TRIES TO RE-INVENT HIMSELF, TELLS BARBER, "MAKE ME LOOK LIKE MOE HOWARD"

PETER COTTONTAIL CRITICALLY WOUNDED BY ROADSIDE BOMB ALONG BAGHDAD BUNNY TRAIL

U.S. military authorities claim beloved rabbit ignored warnings to stay inside the Green Zone

OBAMA SCOLDS *NEW YORKER* MAGAZINE FOR PORTRAYING HIM AS ARAB TERRORIST, ISSUES *FATWA* AGAINST EDITORS

NEW STUDY FINDS WOMEN'S INTELLIGENCE PROPORTIONAL TO SIZE OF THEIR HIPS, INVERSELY PROPORTIONAL TO SIZE OF THEIR CARS

NEW STUDY SUGGESTS LIBERALS ARE "MORE RESPONSIVE TO INFORMATIONAL COMPLEXITY" THAN CONSERVATIVES

Scientists says margin of error is "plus-or-minus Al Sharpton"

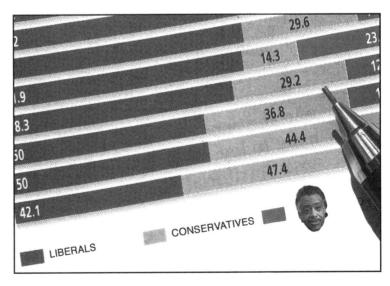

HILLARY CLINTON COLLEGE LETTERS ARE FAKES

Carbon dating suggests forgery; experts say references
to "Lindsay Lohan" and "that cool new iPhone" confirm it

LASER SCANS OF LINCOLN'S HEAD SHOW
SEVERE FACIAL ASSYMETRY, BULLET HOLE

PHARMACEUTICAL COMPANIES BUYING UP AD SPACE ON PATIENTS' GENITALS

NEW YORK - The world-wide publicity generated by the surgeon who snapped a photo of a patient's tattooed genitalia during an operation has prompted drug giant Pfizer to realize it is missing out on a valuable medium to advertise to doctors.

"After years of spending millions of dollars on ads in medical journals and 60-second TV spots, we've concluded we get zero bang for our buck," said Bradleys Roadhouse, spokesman for Pfizer. "To get the doctors' attention, we need to get our name on penises."

Pfizer joins competitors Wyeth, GlaxoSmithKline, and Hoffman-LaRoche in the use of direct-to-physician penis advertising.

Pfizer had been hesitant about jumping on the penis bandwagon but was pushed over the edge by the buzz created when the Mayo Clinic's Dr. Adam Hanser admitted taking a photo of a patient's penis with a tattoo that reads "Hot Rod" and showing it around to other doctors. The incident created an international sensation.

Pfizer would not reveal what it plans to pay the men who advertise for it, but noted that "obviously the more media space we buy, the greater the value to us. In other words: sorry, guys, size matters."

BAGHDAD CHAPTER OF NATIONAL ORGANIZATION FOR WOMEN SAYS FEMALE SUICIDE BOMBER "SHATTERED GLASS CEILING, GLASS WINDOWS, AND GLASS WALLS"

BAGHDAD - The Baghdad Chapter of the National Organization for Women paid homage to the suicide bomber who blew herself up among Shiite pilgrims south of Baghdad yesterday, killing 26. Baghdad NOW issued a statement commending the woman for "shattering the glass ceiling and the glass storefront windows, not to mention the glass doors and car windows several blocks away. In fact, that bomb pretty much shattered everything."

Baghdad NOW bemoaned the fact that when yesterday's suicide bomber entered Paradise, she was greeted by only 55 virgins instead of the 72 that typically greet her male counterparts. A spokeswoman for the organization noted that the Virgin Disparity reflects the gender wage gap that pays women only 77% of what men make for doing the same work.

Baghdad NOW proclaimed they "would not rest" until female suicide bombers received the same afterlife compensation as men.

CLINTON PROPOSAL: TAX NOCTURNAL EMISSIONS TO FUND WOMEN'S SHELTERS

WASHINGTON, D.C. - Senator Hillary Clinton, trailing in the polls for the upcoming California primary and looking to solidify her standing with women voters, proposed a $40 per occurrence tax on nocturnal emissions to fund women's domestic violence shelters. Clinton unveiled the proposal on The Ellen DeGeneres Show today and announced to rousing applause a plan "to eradicate within our lifetime the scourge of any ejaculation, even of the so-called involuntary variety, that occurs without a woman's enthusiastic verbal consent."

Under the Clinton plan, dubbed the "Wet Dream Tax," every teen male, or his parents until he reaches age 18, will automatically be assessed for 15 nocturnal emissions annually. Unmarried males ages 20-27 would be assessed for six occurrences. Some parents of teen boys think the proposed tax is burdensome and discriminatory, especially on top of Clinton's proposed "Masturbation Tax," which would tag every teen male with an annual flat fee of $2,500 to go toward breast cancer research.

A Clinton campaign spokeswoman said the proposed taxes were designed as "compensation for oppression to women since studies show that ejaculatory dreams and fantasies typically involve subjugation and mistreatment of women." She noted that the taxes were not discriminatory, since prospective mothers could control whether to pay them "by utilizing their lawful abortion options and engaging in gender selection" before deciding to give birth to a boy.

Senator Clinton also told Ellen DeGeneres she will take part in this weekend's "Walk to End All Walks Except the Walk for Breast Cancer."

CARBOLICBREAKINGNEWS:

DESPERATE CLINTON CAMPAIGN HIRES MAVERICK FUNDRAISER

Bank of Africa's Dr. Hassan Abu an expert in emailing people for help in transferring money

DESPERATE CLINTON SUPPORTERS "KIDNAP THE NEGRO" IN LAST GASP EFFORT TO SECURE NOMINATION

"If Obama was a white man, he would not be in this position," said Geraldine Ferraro

IDAHO REVISES PLANS FOR ITS COMMEMORATIVE QUARTER; NEW DESIGN TO SALUTE SEN. LARRY CRAIG

NORWEGIAN POLICE FOUND MUNCH MASTERPIECE HIDDEN IN CLOSET BY FOLLOWING ITS MUFFLED SCREAM

OSLO - Norwegian police revealed today how they finally managed to track down Edward Munch's stolen 1893 masterpiece, "The Scream."

According to police spokesman Morten Hojem Ervik, police received a tip last week from a reliable source that the painting, stolen from the Munch Museum in 2004, had been hidden away in the home of wealthy Oslo merchant Bjoern Hoen, who was one of the masterminds of the painting's theft.

On Tuesday, Police searched Hoen's home for seven hours to no avail and were prepared to give up until they heard the faint, muffled scream of the painting coming from a closet on the top floor. It had been hidden away under blankets, and the mouth of its subject had been taped.

Hoen told police that when he stole the painting, he had "no idea how loud and annoying" it would be.

BLUE MAN GROUP WANTED FOR BANK ROBBERY SPREE; EXPLODING BLUE DYE PACKS HIDDEN IN CASH PROVING INEFFECTIVE TO STOP THEM

LAS VEGAS - Las Vegas entertainers *The Blue Man Group* are wanted in a series of bank robberies throughout Nevada. Police say the exploding blue dye packs that banks insert in stolen money are ineffective to stop them.

In theory, when the dye pack explodes, it is supposed to stain the robber, making it easy to identify him. But when the dye pack explodes on the Blue Man Group, no one even notices, and they walk away undetected.

After one recent robbery in downtown Las Vegas, the dye pack exploded seconds after members of the Blue Man Group stepped outside the bank, spewing blue ink all over them. Nevertheless, they continued to walk the streets as if nothing happened, and tourists and passers-by even stopped them for their autographs.

The inability to nab the crooks has left police feeling blue and seeing red.

JOINT CHIEFS' PROBE OF HADITHA CIVILIAN MASSACRE CONCLUDES THAT MARINES COULD USE MORE SENSITIVITY TRAINING

"A kind word, maybe a 'please' and a 'thank you' before shooting civilians, could go a long way toward improving public relations for marines," report concludes

THE 4,000 JEWS WHO FAILED TO SHOW UP FOR WORK AT THE WORLD TRADE CENTER ON SEPTEMBER 11TH ARE SPOTTED SIGHTSEEING IN SAN MARCO

Arabs wonder, "What are those sneaky Jews up to now?"

GIANT ASTEROID STRIKES CARNEGIE MUSEUM'S NEWLY RENOVATED PREHISTORIC EXHIBIT; DINOSAURS DESTROYED ONCE AGAIN

NEIL ARMSTRONG RECEIVES PIECE OF MOON ROCK AT CEREMONY COMMEMORATING THIRTY-FIFTH ANNIVERSARY OF MOON WALK, SAYS HE EXPECTED "SOMETHING MORE"

POPE SCRAPS ANNUAL *URBI ET ORBI* BLESSING IN FAVOR OF CADBURY CREME EGGS

Pontiff startles crowd, says, "Jerry, bring Out the Creme Eggs; I'm done here," then disappears

VATICAN CITY - Pope Benedict XVI scrapped the Pontiff's traditional Easter gift to the world, the *Urbi et Orbi* address, and instead ordered Vatican personnel to pass out tens of thousands of Cadbury Creme Eggs to pilgrims at Saint Peters Square.

Popes typically use their Easter message as an occasion to admonish warring nations to bring an end to bloodshed. This year, the Pope appeared on the balcony at St. Peter's Basilica, but witnesses said he bore a sad and defeated look. He stared at his prepared text in silence for several seconds, causing many in the overflow crowd to assume he was ill. Suddenly he looked up, stared straight ahead, and muttered in a soft but clear voice, "Hopeless, absolutely hopeless." The Pope turned to his right and spoke to someone out of view. "Jerry, bring out the [Cadbury] Creme Eggs. I'm done here." Then he brusquely waved to the crowd and disappeared.

A short time later, a caravan of trucks rolled into Saint Peters Square and began distributing four-packs of the popular Cadbury confections to an estimated 80,000 pilgrims. The Pope has publicly touted Cadbury Creme Eggs, once even singling them out in a speech for their "delicious, soft fondant center."

Later, while downing one of the creme eggs, American tourist Noah Swayne summed up the feelings of many in the crowd, "Sure, I wish he had spoken more. But this was actually better."

SHUFFLEBOARD COURT FOUND ON DECK OF NOAH'S ARK

MOUNT SABALAN, IRAN - An archeological expedition to Iran's Mount Sabalan has discovered a massive seafaring vessel dating from 2400 BC, constructed of cypress wood and measuring 450 feet long with a gross volume of 1.5 million cubic feet. Scientists say that based on the age, size, and composition of the structure, it can only be Noah's Ark.

But the most surprising feature of the ark, said expedition director Dr. Hadley V. Baxendale, is the 39-by-6-foot shuffleboard court found on its main deck. The court is laid out in the exact dimensions of a present day, regulation-sized deck shuffleboard court.

Dr. Baxendale said his team also believes it has uncovered evidence that the occupants of the ark engaged in the practice of reserving chairs next to the swimming pool by laying towels on them.

NEWLY DISCOVERED NOSTRADAMUS PREDICTION PROVES HE WAS A PROPHET: "IN THE FUTURE, PEOPLE WILL CONSIDER ME A FRAUD"

NEW YORK - Nostradamus enthusiasts claim to have discovered the proof-positive that has long eluded them to show that the controversial prophet was not a fraud.

The seer's devotees say they have uncovered a long-lost writing of the mysterious prophet predicting that people in the centuries following his death would regard him as a hoax -- which is exactly what has happened. "He was right on the mark," said Bradleys Roadhouse, President of the International Nostradamus Society. "Only Nostradamus could have predicted that one."

The newly-discovered "Quatrain of Nostradamus" reads as follows:

A great clamor will be heard on the plains of man,
and the multitudes will strike at the good one,
and he will be reviled, though his words are true,
and the people will be caught in the wheels of a giant machine -- turning, turning, turning endlessly.

"That's about as clear as a prediction could be," said Roadhouse. "What further proof could we possibly provide these skeptics?"

According to Roadhouse, the newly discovered writing not only contains Nostradamus' prediction about his own skeptics, but it also foretells the rise of a mechanized society.

CARBOLICBREAKINGNEWS:

"BLT KILLER" SMEARED MAYONNAISE ON HIS VICTIMS BEFORE HE MURDERED THEM

FRANKENSTEIN MONSTER ASSAULTED IN CONVENIENCE STORE

Horror icon "mortified" by incident; police say no monster has even been publicly assaulted except by another monster or a pitchfork-wielding mob

SCIENTISTS CAN'T LOCATE 96% OF MATTER IN UNIVERSE, SUMMON FORMER U.N. ARMS INSPECTOR HANS BLIX TO FIND IT

WASHINGTON, D.C. - Scientists trying to create a detailed inventory of all the matter and energy in the cosmos have run into a curious problem -- the vast majority of it is missing. Only 4 percent of the matter and energy in the universe has been found; the other 96 percent remains elusive.

But not for long. Scientists have called Hans Blix, the former chief UN arms inspector who found no evidence that Saddam Hussein harbored weapons of mass destruction, out of retirement to find the missing matter.

Blix says he's going to do what he does best. "If the missing matter isn't there, don't worry, I won't find it. I'm the world's foremost authority on not finding things that aren't there."

President Bush did not hide his displeasure with the appointment. "That fool couldn't find his [penis] if his life depended on it," Bush said. The President announced that the United States plans to take action on its own concerning the missing matter without awaiting Blix's findings.

"I will get the man who did this," Bush vowed.

5.4-MAGNITUDE QUAKE FELT LIKE 13.7 INSIDE *EARTHQUAKE* RIDE

LOS ANGELES - A 5.4 magnitude earthquake struck Southern California yesterday afternoon, killing 162 people on the *Earthquake* Thrill Ride at Universal Studios Hollywood.

Outside the *Earthquake* attraction, the quake caused only moderate damage and no serious injuries, but inside the attraction, which simulates an 8.3-magnitude quake, the combination of the real and simulated quakes produced a 13.7-magnitude quake, the highest ever recorded. The previous most powerful earthquake was a 9.6-magnitude quake in Chile in 1960.

One eyewitness said the remains of the riders trapped in the attraction "looked more like pudding than human beings." They were scooped up and carried out in buckets as thousands of curious riders cued up in lines to enter the attraction. One park official said the tragedy may give the ride, one of the park's oldest, some much-needed cachet. "We're hoping we can get a bounce like Universal's *Twister* attraction did a few years back, when the ride and a real tornado combined to produce that historic F10."

OBAMA CAMPAIGN RELEASES FIRST
IN A SERIES OF MOTIVATIONAL POSTERS

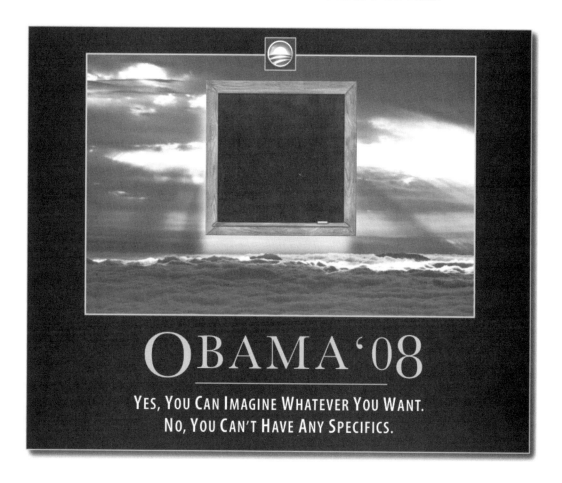

CARBOLICBREAKING**NEWS:**

CLINTON VICTORY IN PENNSYLVANIA PRIMARY ATTRIBUTED TO MIRACLE OF MONICA LEWINSKY'S DRESS

Face of Eleanor Roosevelt appears in semen stain; Clinton supporters call it "a sign"

BUSH VOWS TO PREVENT IRAN FROM BUILDING ATOMIC FIREBALLS CANDY FACTORY

CARBOLICSMOKEBALL

presents

ZOMBIES ATE MY LOCAL NEWS

UNIVERSITY OF PITTSBURGH'S LAST MALE UNDERGRADUATE DROPS OUT

PITTSBURGH - Edward Johnson, 19, the last male undergraduate student enrolled at the University of Pittsburgh, dropped out of college this morning to work full-time at his brother-in-law's pizza shop.

Johnson's departure is consistent with a national trend some are calling an epidemic that sees women far outnumbering men on college campuses. At the University of Pittsburgh, there are now 17,246 female undergrads and zero males.

"I didn't catch on until long after my buds that studying's just not cool, dude," Johnson told a reporter. "I can make too much money delivering [pizza] to bother with school. Plus, since I'm paid in cash, I won't have to pay tax on it." Johnson smiled sheepishly. "Dropping out [of college] leaves me more time to do what my boys are doing," he explained, "-- play video games and [masturbate] to Internet porn." (Johnson later contacted this reporter to request omission of his statement about not paying taxes.)

Several student residents at Litchfield Towers, Johnson's former dormitory, said his departure is not welcome news. "The women are definitely going to miss having Johnson," said sophomore Carla Vango. Vanessa McBride, 19, lamented: "This used to be a co-ed dorm. Without Ed, it's just a 'co' dorm." Dorothy Buumulak, President of Pitt's "SARM," *Students Against Rape and Men*, is also unhappy: "It's a major loss, because as long as he was here, in the back of my mind, I knew our women had someone to accuse of sexual assault," she said. "Fortunately, we can still rely on the theory of 'recovered memories' to blame Pitt's former male student population for past assaults. But Pitt's administration needs to make a concerted effort to recruit a new crop of males."

In the lobby of the dorm, a harried Dean of Students Velveeta Hyphen-Lugosi curtly stated that the administration is "making every effort" to attract more male students. "Oh, yes, we definitely want that, that gender balance thing," Hyphen-Lugosi said, rolling her eyes. Hyphen-Lugosi interrupted the interview to address a mover passing through the lobby pushing a cart filled with urinals. "Make sure you remove every last one of those f***ing things. If I see one of them anywhere in the building, I'll have your [cajones] for breakfast."

Hyphen-Lugosi was asked what Pitt would do to make males feel more welcome. "For one thing, we'll make their course-load more male-friendly," she said. "In our required course, 'Historical Atrocities of the Patriarchy Against Women,' we're going to serve free beer and allow them to sit behind a black curtain in the back of the room."

LOCAL MAN WANTS TO SET TIMETABLE FOR WITHDRAWAL FROM FAMILY REUNION; WIFE RESISTS, SAYS EARLY PULL-OUT COULD LEAD TO CHAOS

BROOKLYN - David Corbett is insisting that his wife Barbara set a firm time-table for withdrawal from her family reunion this Sunday. Mr. Corbett expressed his concerns on the subject over breakfast yesterday morning.

"We simply cannot go into this thing without an exit strategy," he said. "We've got to get in and get out with as little collateral damage as possible."

Mrs. Corbett refused to budge: "We're going to be there for as long as it takes."

In the opinion of Mr. Corbett and several in-laws he has consulted, it is likely he could get bogged down in a quagmire, especially if he allows himself to get drawn into an internecine squabble over the merits of using Miracle Whip over mayonnaise in the preparation of the potato salad.

Mr. Corbett admits he is nervous. "We're going in with the best of intentions. But that's not enough. We need a well-defined plan, and we need to realize there are limits to what we can accomplish."

Mr. Corbett argued that maintaining an open-ended presence at the reunion would be counter-productive. "They're going to think we enjoy these things, and then they'll want to have another one next year."

His wife, however, was reluctant to set a firm timetable for departure. "I'm worried that if we leave early, there could be violence."

Mrs. Corbett said long-simmering tensions and factional rivalries could explode without the presence of a peace-keeping force.

"You have to realize there's going to be an enormous amount of alcohol consumed," she said.

CARBOLICBREAKINGNEWS:

RAPIST APPREHENDED; NAMES OF VICTIMS, NICKNAME OF PENIS BEING WITHHELD BY POLICE

OUTCRY OVER REDESIGNED TRAFFIC SIGN

Men's rights advocates ask, "Why do traffic signs always depict the male holding the gun?"

TEAM INVESTIGATING HOW "ADULT NOVELTY" WAS LAUNCHED INTO CROWD DURING HOT DOG SHOOT

PITTSBURGH - Mr. and Mrs. Bradleys Roadhouse, seated in Section 9, Row F, near the visitors dugout at PNC Park during Saturday night's game between the Pittsburgh Pirates and Cincinnati Reds, got an unwanted surprise in the fourth inning. That's the inning the Pirate Parrot traditionally launches tightly packed hot dogs into the crowd from his "hot dog shooter," which resembles a hand-held cannon. For reasons the Pirates are still investigating, the Parrot shot more than hot dogs at Saturday night's game.

Pirates General Manager Dave Littlefield issued a prepared statement that explained what happened: "The Pirates deeply regret that somehow during our popular hot-dog-shoot launch last Saturday, several simulated novelty male organs were launched into the stands instead of our usual plump, all-beef franks. An examination of the offending items revealed that they were of the kosher variety, partially skinless. We are cognizant of and deeply regret the trauma this incident may have caused families who came to PNC Park for wholesome entertainment, as well as those male recipients of the item who don't quite measure up. The Pirates are investigating this matter."

A flushed Mrs. Roadhouse described what happened: "I don't eat 'hot dogs' for religious reasons, but I do enjoy watching the Parrot shoot off a frankfurter now and again. On this particular occasion, he cocked his cannon, and it spewed something into the air. The next thing I knew, I was looking down into my husband's lap and seeing something I knew didn't belong there: a large package. I reached over and grabbed what I thought was a hot dog."

Although Mrs. Roadhouse claimed to be mortified, her husband said "she took particular delight in whipping that monster out of its wrapper."

That wasn't the only snafu during the game. Later, during the t-shirt toss, some fans received female underwear instead of the usual t-shirt. 80-year-old usher Hank Sepp passed out when he caught a glimpse of what had been tossed to the crowd. The culprits of this prank turned out to be the the the slingshot shooters. "We were in the changing room before the game," explained ballgirl Velveeta Lugosi, "and I go, 'Like, let's shoot off our panties tonight,' and the other girls go, 'Like, 'OK.'"

Mr. Littlefield said that the female underwear incident "was just an innocent prank" that warrants no disciplinary action. In fact, the Pirates are considering repeating it at future games.

FEMINIST CONDEMNS BOY WHO CUTS HER GRASS FOR IGNORING WOMEN'S INTERPRETATIONS OF THEIR OWN EXPERIENCES

BALTIMORE, MD - Local feminist Noelle Swayne is complaining that the young man who cuts her grass, Adam Hermann, 14, cut it too short last week. Adam denies it, and Swayne is so angry she fired him.

Adam, who'd been cutting Ms. Swayne's grass for two years, claims he "had the mower on the same setting I always use." But Ms. Swayne rejected Adam's claim as "invalid," because "it ignores a woman's interpretation of her own experiences."

"Adam is speaking from a perspective of male privilege," Ms. Swayne said angrily. "As an exponent of patriarchy, of course he will say whatever pops into his head to preserve his male entitlements if he thinks they're being taken from him." Ms. Swayne said she will fire Adam and hire a female grass cutter "who, incidentally, makes only 77 cents for every dollar Adam makes."

Adam has a different take on it. "Ms. Swayne's pretending she's upset with me because the woman she lives with caught her staring at me when I was cutting the grass without my shirt," he said. "I think Ms. Swayne, like, has a crush on me. Anyway, this isn't about male privilege or patriarchy; it's about the setting on the lawnmower's blade, which was exactly right. And by the way, if she could have found some girl to cut the grass at 77% of what she pays me, that cheap b*tch would've done it two years ago."

LOCAL WOMAN CALLS HUSBAND'S DEATH FROM HEART ATTACK AFTER LIFETIME OF OVEREATING "JUST THE WAKE UP CALL HE NEEDED"

PLEASANT HILLS, PA - Vera Marcal said her husband's death from chronic heart disease last week was "just the wake-up call he needed" after a lifetime of overeating. Julius Marcal, 48, of Pleasant Hills died last week after suffering his second heart attack in the past two years.

"I've been after him to lose weight for years," Mrs. Marcal gloated. "When I saw him clutching his chest, I knew this was just the thing he needed to put an end to those bad habits. Some people have to be hit over the head, you know."

Mr. Marcal was buried from St. Elizabeth's Church following a funeral Saturday.

LOCAL MAN: "THE ONLY TIME I FEEL ALIVE IS WHEN I'M WEARING MY COLLAR BOMB"

BUFFALO - Local man and *bon vivant* Noah Swayne of Orchard Park revealed that he "doesn't feel alive" unless his triple-banded metal collar bomb is securely locked around his neck.

"First thing I do when I come home from work is slap on the collar [bomb]," said Swayne. "I know the neighbors must think it's strange seeing me cutting the grass wearing the collar, but I'm one of those guys who's always lived a sort of high-octane life."

Swayne insists on setting the timer to detonate the bomb while he's wearing

the collar. "Only one time did I come close to having it go off -- when I accidentally fell asleep," he chuckles. "I disarmed it with seven seconds to spare."

Swayne confides that he sometimes wears the collar to bed. "Many a night my wife assumes the bomb went off," he winks. "Every couple should add one of these to their lovemaking regimen."

GABE KOTTER, BELOVED TEACHER WHO GAVE "LAST LECTURE" THAT INSPIRED MILLIONS, BEATEN TO DEATH BY HIS STUDENTS

BROOKLYN - Gabe Kotter, a teenage troublemaker who returned to his former high school to teach a new generation of delinquents and wrote a best-selling book based on his "last lecture," was beaten to death by a gang of former students yesterday.

Police have arrested Arnold Horshack of Fire Island, Vinnie Barbarino of Bensonhurst, homeless man Frederick Washington, and Juan Epstein of the East Side, and charged them with first degree murder. Authorities said the men were taught by Mr. Kotter over twenty-five years ago. School records reveal that none of the suspects graduated. Detective Mike Maloney said the men confessed that they were jealous of the notoriety Mr. Kotter had achieved following the news that he was terminally ill.

"Mr. Kotter made us sit through corny speeches every day," Mr. Washington said in a statement to police. "He bored the hell out of us so bad we all dropped out. We didn't want him doing that to other kids."

MAN IMPERSONATING VICE-PRESIDENT PULLS OVER WOMAN ON PARKWAY WEST

PITTSBURGH - A man claiming to be Vice-President Dick Cheney pulled a woman over just off the Perrysville Exit on Interstate 279 yesterday and asked her to join him for an evening of "intense discussions on the future of Iraq and intercourse."

Mary O'Neill, 34, was heading towards Cranberry in the right lane when a black sedan pulled into the passing lane beside her with a portable flashing light atop it. "At that point, the driver began beeping his horn repeatedly and motioned for me to wind down my window," said Ms. O'Neill. "Then I saw him put what appeared to be a bullhorn to his mouth, and he said, 'This is the Vice-President of the United States of America. Please pull off to the side of the road.' Well, naturally, when the Vice-President asks you to do that, you do."

Ms. O'Neill put her car in park, and the driver of the sedan approached her. "I've been following you all night," he said. "Please don't cut and run. In the interest of national security, I'd like you to join me at an undisclosed location. I have a weapon of mass destruction in my trousers. Hans Blix couldn't find it; the French couldn't find it. Only you can find it. And when you do, I will fill you with shock and awe. Best of all, I will set no timetable for withdrawal."

The man then offered Ms. O'Neill a no-bid contract on love.

Ms. O'Neill said she became skeptical of the man's claim to be the Vice-President when it dawned on her that a high-ranking government official probably would not be driving his own car, so she sped away to the Ross Police Department.

The suspect, a black male in his mid-twenties, medium build, with two gold teeth, is still at large. Anyone with information is asked to contact the Ross Police.

CARBOLICBREAKINGNEWS:

ST. PATRICK'S DAY PARADE MARRED BY SOBRIETY, MARCHERS WALKING IN STRAIGHT LINES

MRS. NOAH SWAYNE MAKES WISH, BLOWS OUT CANDLES; HUSBAND'S PENIS DISAPPEARS

CATHEDRAL OF LEARNING UNDERGOES CONTROVERSIAL FORESKIN RESTORATION

SUBURBANITES NOW CHOOSING SHRUBBERY OVER SECURITY

37 million American homeowners now living in *irri*gated communities.

LOCAL MAN SUES J.C. PENNEY, CLAIMS MEN'S UNDERWEAR AD ON PAGE 6 OF SUNDAY'S FLYER TURNED HIM GAY

LOCAL CATHOLIC MAN RETRACTS SIGN OF PEACE

PITTSBURGH - Immediately following the 9:30 a.m. mass at St. Elizabeth Church in suburban Pittsburgh on Sunday, Noah Swayne announced to fellow parishioners that he was retracting the sign of peace he had given to an unnamed parishioner.

Swayne addressed about a half-dozen parishioners on the steps of the church. "I regret to announce that on my way out of church, I was informed by a reliable source that a certain person to whom I had given the sign of peace, whose name I will not reveal, is rumored to have engaged in certain misconduct that I will not elaborate upon," Swayne explained. "Accordingly, in good conscience, I can't allow the sign of peace to stand."

This is not the first time Swayne has retracted the sign of peace. He did the same thing last January to his nephew, 16-year-old Matt Swayne, after learning that Matt's father had caught him masturbating to a *Penthouse* Magazine. At the time, Swayne also said that he would never shake Matt's hand again, "for obvious reasons."

For his latest retraction, Swayne said he would consider reinstating the sign of peace if the unspecified misconduct were rectified.

DULL MAN ELATED HE'S BEEN NAMED "PERSON OF INTEREST" IN ONGOING CRIMINAL INVESTIGATION

PITTSBURGH - Hadley V. Baxendale is being called a person of interest in the embezzlement of almost $20,000 from his former employer, Bradleys Roadhouse Bar and Grill in Pleasant Hills, where Baxendale worked as an office manager and waiter for six years until he was discharged in December 2006 for accounting irregularities.

"He's just so excited," said Baxendale's wife Maria. "He's always been on the quiet side, and nobody's ever said he was 'of interest,' until now."

"Chalk this one up for the little guys, the guys everybody wrote off as dull or boring," Baxendale proudly said from his cell at the County Jail. "I have a warrant here that says I'm not dull, I'm not boring."

"I'm a 'Person of interest!' Don't you just love the sound of that?" he added.

SHAKEN ANDY WARHOL MUSEUM CURATOR FINDS STASH OF DOG-EARED *PLAYBOY* MAGAZINES IN ARTIST'S PERSONAL COLLECTION

"But he was a flaming homosexual, I swear!" sobs curator Tom Sokolowski; museum's cultural and intellectual cachet destroyed

LOCAL MAN INCENSED: VERNAL EQUINOX "ISN'T WHAT IT USED TO BE"

PITTSBURGH - Popular *bon vivant* Noah Swayne is spearheading a petition drive to express his "extreme displeasure" that the temperatures for the first days of spring feel more like winter.

"Somebody needs to take a stand on this," Swayne explained.

"I tell every child I come across, 'You should have seen the vernal equinox in the old days. It came roaring in like thunder and hit us like a great wave of balmy bliss.'"

Swayne said his next protest will be over Christmas, "because that's not as good as it used to be, either."

HOMEOWNER GETS VERDICT IN SUIT AGAINST PAINTER WHO USED TWO DIFFERENT SHADES OF WHITE ON WALLS

Difference in shades of white not discernible to average person, but case assigned to Eskimo Judge Canku, who can discern hundreds of shades of white

PITTSBURGH - Karl Swayne sued his house painter, Bradleys Roadhouse Paints, because, according to the complaint, "the defendant contracted with plaintiff to paint the walls of plaintiff's luxury home all 'white,' but defendant proceeded to paint the walls utilizing different shades of white, contrary to both the parties' agreement and reasonable industry standards."

The plaintiff seemed to suffer an insurmountable blow to his case when he admitted in his deposition that he could not tell the difference in the shades of paint utilized. "It all just looked 'white' to me," he testified. But fate smiled on the plaintiff. When the case was called for trial, the jurist assigned to it was Judge Noah Canku, who claims to be "100% Eskimo, and therefore capable of discerning several hundred different shades of white."

After viewing the walls for less than three seconds, Judge Canku said he found the paint job "appalling -- it hurts my eyes to look at it," and he awarded the plaintiff $4,300, the cost to repaint the walls.

CARBOLICBREAKINGNEWS:

WOMAN WHO STIMULATED BOYFRIEND TO EXCESS IS FIRST REPORTED CASE OF SECOND-HAND BLINDNESS

MORTGAGE DEADBEAT APOLOGIZES FOR SUB-PRIME MORTGAGE CRISIS

PITTSBURGH - Velveeta Lugosi-Swayne hasn't slept well in three weeks. She feels the weight of the financial world on her shoulders, due to the crisis on Wall Street stemming from the collapse of the sub-prime mortgage industry.

"I was one of these people who shouldn't have been given a mortgage because of my poor credit history," said Lugosi-Swayne. "But they gave me one anyway, and I've been missing payments for months." Lugosi-Swayne wipes her eyes with a Kleenex. "But I'm not worried about me. Let them take my house, I don't care. I'm worried about the disruption I've caused to the world-wide economy."

Swayne's admissions come as foreclosure filings have reached epidemic proportions. Analysts say that the fallout from mortgages gone bad is spreading well beyond borrowers in default and is effecting numerous other aspects of the economy.

"I can't tell you how bad I feel about it," said Lugosi-Swayne, choking back tears. "I can only hope the American people find it in their hearts to forgive me."

CITY DENIES NEW PEDESTRIAN CROSSING SIGN SHOWS CONTEMPT FOR WALKERS

PHILADELPHIA, PA - Philadelphia Mayor Michael Nutter today reiterated his stance that the city's new pedestrian crossing signs "are not vulgar" and "do not, in any way, show contempt for pedestrians."

Nutter explained that the signs reflect a "time-honored tradition" in the City of Brotherly Love, and that they "merely extend the same courtesy pedestrians, and especially tourists, have always received in Philadelphia."

LOCAL MAN REALIZES WHAT'S BEEN MISSING FROM HIS LIFE: AN OBTRUSIVE SOUNDTRACK

PITTSBURGH - All his life, Noah Swayne, 22, could never tell how he was supposed to feel about or react to any given situation. Now he knows why.

"It was, like, obvious, dude, but for 22 years I didn't get it," said Swayne. "There's no soundtrack in my life. No matter what happens to me, I can never be totally sure if it's exciting or sad or scary or what."

Swayne realized what was missing last weekend when he and his girlfriend went to see *Beowulf*. "I knew exactly how I was supposed to feel, because the music told me," he explained. "Hell, if it weren't for the music swelling in the background, who would have realized Indiana Jones' life was so f***ing exciting or that Elliott was sad when ET left him?"

Swayne is finally doing something about it. He wrote to iconic movie composer John Williams and asked him to write a Noah Swayne theme song. "I gave Mr. Williams some details about my life he can use to create an appropriate theme, you know, like when they took the paper route away from me because Mrs. Manion claimed I unzipped myself in front of her daughter; and when me and Jimmy Modesta invented the time machine, and it actually worked for a brief time; and how my sister accused me of, like, doing something to her, but it was totally consensual." To date, Williams has not responded, but Swayne points out "he's a very, very busy man. It takes a tremendous amount of time to write all those notes on the music paper and everything."

DRIVER PICKS UP WRONG "POPE BENEDICT" AT AIRPORT

WASHINGTON, D.C. - Limousine driver Noah Swayne, assigned to pick up Pope Benedict at Reagan National Airport on the Pontiff's U.S. visit, accidentally picked up the wrong man – ironically another traveler also named "Pope Benedict."

"I waited at the baggage area, holding up my 'Pope Benedict' sign," Swayne explained, "and this man approached me and said, 'I'm Mr. Benedict.' It was the weirdest thing – turns out his first name is 'Pope,' too."

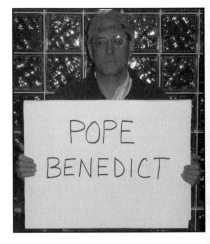

It wasn't until they were on the road that Swayne learned his passenger is not the head of the Roman Catholic Church but a Radio Shack store manager from Alexandria.

Pope Benedict XVI of the Vatican was forced to share a cab from the airport with comedian Carrot Top.

MURAL FULFILLS TERMS OF ANDREW CARNEGIE'S WILL

"I direct that my likeness shall appear atop a hot dog shop,
wearing curlers and sitting under a hair dryer, next to a pop artist
of indeterminate sexuality, while soaking my hands for a manicure."

SNOWSTORM TRAPS CHANNEL ELEVEN NEWS TEAM IN STUDIO; ANCHORS RESORT TO CANNIBALISM

Anchor David Johnson broadcasts urgent plea for help, hair products

PITTSBURGH - A sudden winter storm caught forecasters by surprise last night, rendering many roads too hazardous to travel and creating a crisis at a local television station. Shortly after 8pm, WPXI broke in to regularly scheduled programming to announce that the station was completely surrounded by snow and that employees had no way of leaving.

A crawl across the bottom of the screen announced that some of the on-air talent had become so desperate for food that they were resorting to cannibalism and debating the best way to prepare reporter Alan Jennings for human consumption.

Anchorman David Johnson asked for the prayers of all viewers and urged local government officials to ready plans for an emergency airdrop of badly needed hair-care products. "Things are getting desperate, folks," he warned. "A little more than an hour ago, I saw some gray."

FIVE-BLOCK AREA AROUND MAYOR'S PANTS CORDONED OFF DUE TO APPEARANCE OF "SUSPICIOUS PACKAGE"

CHICAGO - Chicago police blocked off the area around the corner of N. LaSalle and W. Washington Streets this morning after authorities were notified of a suspicious package found in the region of Mayor Richard M. Daley's crotch. Bomb technicians on the scene speculated it could have been explosives, or that it might have come from a particularly stiff wind blowing off Lake Michigan.

Deputy Sean Cannon, who serves writs for the Sheriff's Office, noticed the package as the mayor walked down N. LaSalle Street around 8 a.m. Cannon asked this reporter to note that he "wasn't purposefully looking at the mayor's crotch area, just as I wouldn't look at any man's crotch area. I just sort of glanced at him and it was pretty hard -- that is, it was pretty hard to miss."

Fellow deputies secured the scene, moving children several blocks away and charging other bystanders admission.

The mayor's Chief of Staff Lori Healey issued the following statement: "Wow! Can that Dick fill out his pants, or what!"

FOX'S PIZZA IN BALDWIN, PA SAYS IT WILL RELEASE "GUT-WRENCHING" TAPES OF SEPTEMBER 11TH TELEPHONE ORDERS

In one emotional call, customer said: "Wow, you should see what they're showing on TV, man! Can I have a large with sausage and pepperoni to go?"

PITTSBURGH - Ron Jones, owner of Fox's Pizza in Baldwin, said today he will release the tapes of telephone orders at his pizza shop from September 11, 2001.

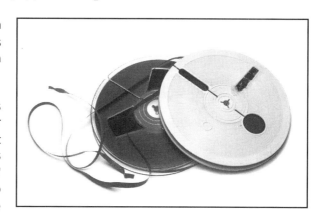

"I've steadfastly refused to release these tapes for six years," Jones said, "because of their grueling content" relating to the terrorist attacks on New York and Washington. He says he has reconsidered in light of the tapes' "extraordinary historical significance," not to mention a book he is writing based on the tapes that he expects will bring him a "tidy payday."

None of the callers on the tapes had any connection to the World Trade Center; all of them made the calls from Western Pennsylvania. But Jones insists a few of the calls contain "indirect, oblique but implied references" to the terrorist attacks that were occurring that day, and thus "provide a window into the souls of the terrorists."

On one of the calls, a male caller is heard to say, "You should see what they're showing on TV, dude [referring to the World Trade Center attacks]. Wow! Can I have a large with pepperoni and sausage to go?" Jones refers to that call as "spine-tingling." A female caller is heard to ask: "Did you see the TV? I was just in New York last summer, and boy am I glad I'm not there now."

Several callers asked, "Do you deliver?"

Jones predicts the "gut-wrenching calls" will be studied by scholars "for centuries to come." An informal poll shows the public is divided as to whether the tapes should be released. Melissa Lugosi-Bloomberg of Baldwin echoed the majority: "The real question is, why did they record those calls in the first place? And then why did they save them?"

*CARBOLIC*BREAKING*NEWS:*

HIGH SCHOOL BOYS PROTEST LACK OF SEX SCANDALS THIS SEMESTER, DEMAND MORE FEMALE TEACHERS TRY TO SEDUCE THEM

LOCAL TEEN "PISSED" HE FORGOT ALL ABOUT KWANZA THIS YEAR

"I don't know what I'm going to do," said Noah Swayne, Jr.
of White Oak. "It's pretty damned serious!"

LOCAL WOMAN SUES KENTUCKY DERBY FOR STEALING THE CATCHPHRASE FROM HER WEDDING NIGHT: "THE MOST EXCITING TWO MINUTES IN SPORTS"

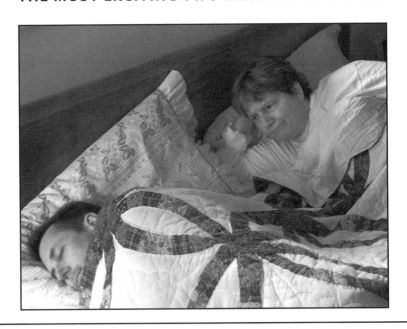

PARTICIPANTS IN CHARITY WALK TO END
DISORIENTATION GET CONFUSED, LOST

FIRST MASS JITTERS: NEW BISHOP MISSPEAKS, URGES
PARISHIONERS TO GIVE EACH OTHER "SIGN OF WAR"

LOCAL MAN TELLS "F*CKING TWICE-A-YEAR CATHOLICS": NEVER AGAIN CLUTTER MY CHURCH ON EASTER

PITTSBURGH - Noah Swayne, 43, has a message for Catholics who only attend mass on Christmas and Easter: "Keep your f*cking, sorry asses out of my church from now on." Swayne was outraged on Easter Sunday when there were approximately four times the number of regular worshippers at church.

Swayne, a long-time parishioner at St. Elizabeth's in Pleasant Hills, says the "interlopers" are easy to spot. "They're usually better dressed than the regulars, because they obviously don't realize that Catholics don't bother to don the fancy garb of commerce like the Protestants and the Jews who are all out trying to impress one another." Moreover, according to Swayne, "they don't know the prayers" and just stand there "like f*cking zombies."

Swayne notes that none of this stops the "interlopers" from stealing his regular pew, eighth pew on the left at the 7:30 Mass, or from receiving Holy Communion. Swayne makes sure to tell them exactly how he feels during the sign of peace. "Yesterday, for example, I shook one interloper's hand and told her that I hate her with every fiber of my being."

Swayne says he's only doing the Lord's work. "I'm just sort of God's back-up in case he doesn't realize he has hypocrites in his midst."

THREE LOCAL MEN CASTRATED DURING CLINTON RALLY

PITTSBURGH - Three men were castrated during Monday's Market Square rally for Hillary Clinton, bringing the total number of men neutered at Clinton rallies nationwide since the presidential campaign began to 29. This news outlet does not identify victims of castrations at Clinton rallies.

"It was scary when word about the three guys spread through the crowd," said Clinton supporter Noah Swayne, 22. "We all figured that the guys who got snipped must have been asking for it."

Lt. Governor Catherine Baker Knoll explained that men need to be vigilant at Clinton rallies. "They shouldn't walk alone, and they should be accompanied by a woman at all times," said the Lt. Governor. "I don't want to say these three particular dudes asked for it, but these three particular dudes probably did ask for it," she explained. "They probably can't stand women," she smirked. "I'm only kidding about that last part -- it's just something we say in the Clinton campaign to pass the time."

ON LAST NIGHT'S BROADCAST, NEW WEATHER CHANNEL METEOROLOGIST MIKHAIL GORBACHEV SHOWS PATH OF MONSTER STORM SWEEPING ACROSS PENNSYLVANIA

UNIVERSITY OF PITTSBURGH TO GIVE AWAY iPOD FOR EVERY SEXUAL ASSAULT COMPLAINT IN EFFORT TO INCREASE "EMBARRASSINGLY LOW" CAMPUS RAPE STATISTICS

PITTSBURGH - Velveeta Swayne-Lugosi, coordinator of the University of Pittsburgh's Office of Sexual Assault Services, announced that starting immediately the University will give away a free iPod to every female on campus who reports a sexual assault. "It is our hope that women subjected to brutal rapes will be able to enjoy their iPod Classic, with up to 160 GB of storage, throughout the entire medical, judicial, and recovery ordeal."

The giveaway is designed to increase Pitt's historically low sexual assault numbers. "There is a campus rape epidemic in America, except that the victims themselves don't know about it," explained Ms. Swayne-Lugosi. In 2006, of all the crimes reported to Pitt's campus police, there was just one report of an on-campus sexual assault of any kind, compared to 32 burglaries and 120 liquor law violations. "One would think with so many liquor law violations, we would have far more sexual assaults, but sadly that's not the case," said Ms. Swayne-Lugosi.

Ms. Swayne-Lugosi chronicled the chilling facts about campus rape. "Rape is the most underreported of all crimes. We know it's underreported because no one is reporting all these rapes that we know must be occurring. Which proves, of course, how rampant rape really is on campus. We think the free iPod will encourage those women who like to listen to good music and who have been brutally raped, usually by a formerly trusted and loyal male friend or classmate, to come forward."

Ms. Swayne-Lugosi discounted the concerns of male students that the giveaway might encourage false accusations. "That's the whole idea, Einstein," she said. After a short pause she added, "Please don't print that."

And what if free iPods don't get the numbers up? "Well, given the number of burglaries on campus, maybe we'll have to think about changing our radical feminist mantra from 'All men are rapists' to 'All men are burglars.'"

PENNSYLVANIA GOVERNOR UNDER FIRE FOR FAILING TO CHECK INTO BACKGROUND OF NEW GAMING CONTROL BOARD CHAIRMAN

Alphonse Gabriel Capone said to have "ties" to organized crime.

HARRISBURG - Governor Edward G. Rendell is smarting over the flap caused by his administration's failure to do a rudimentary check into the background of the new head of the state Gaming Control Board, Alphonse Gabriel Capone, also known as 'Scarface," "boss," and "kingpin."

When the Rendell administration picked Capone, who donated in excess of $600,000 to Rendell's re-election bid, it failed to ask him if he had a criminal record. Capone has been linked to gangland killings and been convicted in connection with both illegal alcohol trafficking and bribes of government officials.

Capone, reached at his cell at the Alcatraz Federal Penitentiary, said the allegations were "more of the same." He deferred further questions to his associate and vice-chair of the Gaming Control Board, gangster Frank Nitti.

Rendell told reporters he was not concerned about Capone's failure to make full disclosure. "Oh, I can't get excited about that; this is all just another Republican witch hunt," Rendell said. "I mean, the way you guys [the press] twist things, it's understandable that accomplished people like Al [Capone] don't want to reveal every single incident, no matter how innocuous, from their past," Rendell said.

Lt. Governor Catherine Baker Knoll, who is prone to referring to Governor Edward G. Rendell as "Edward G. Robinson," the late actor who played mobsters in the movies, told reporters, "now Pennsylvania has two gangsters in high places, the Governor and Scarface."

CARBOLICBREAKINGNEWS:

STUTTERING CAROLER REPEATS THE SOUNDING JOY, RUINS CHRISTMAS CONCERT

SALVATION ARMY BELL-RINGER MAULED BY SALIVATING HOUNDS; PAVLOV DENIES RESPONSIBILITY

RADIO SHACK ROBBERY THWARTED WHEN THIEF WAS DELAYED GIVING CLERK HIS ZIP CODE

MULTIPLE, "PERHAPS INNUMERABLE," NUMBERS TO BE ADDED TO 9-1-1 EMERGENCY PHONE NUMBER

UPSET PARENTS SPEAK OUT AFTER RESCUERS EXTRACT THREE-YEAR-OLD GIRL FROM 50-FOOT WELL: "THAT'S NOT HER!"

RESPONSE TO PROFESSOR RANDY PAUSCH'S "LAST LECTURE" SO GREAT, CARNEGIE MELLON UNIVERSITY ADMINISTRATORS URGING MORE FACULTY MEMBERS TO BECOME TERMINALLY ILL

INTERCOURSE, PENNSYLVANIA'S PROGRESSIVE AMISH WANT TO UPDATE TOWN'S QUAINT IMAGE BY OFFICIALLY CHANGING ITS NAME TO "F*CK, PENNSYLVANIA"

FRANK LLOYD WRIGHT'S PRECURSOR TO "FALLINGWATER" WAS HOUSE BUILT ATOP MINE FIRE CALLED "BURNINGHOUSE"

Wright decided fire "wasn't the way to go" when he saw his first masterpiece "burn to a crsip" in less than an hour

CENTRALIA, PA - It is the stuff of legend how acclaimed architect Frank Lloyd Wright jump-started his moribund career in 1937 at the age of 69 by designing a house perched over a Western Pennsylvania waterfall for Pittsburgh department store magnate Edgar Kaufmann. Fallingwater remains one of the most celebrated private residences in the world. Not so well known is Wright's precursor to Fallingwater, designed for Kaufmann a few years earlier, which Wright built directly atop an underground coal mine fire.

"Mr. Wright thought this would create a perpetual smoldering effect in the residence," explained Wright scholar Professor Franklin Toker.

In keeping with the tradition of lending pithy monikers to Wright homes, the architect dubbed that creation Burninghouse.

But just fifty-eight minutes after it was constructed, Burninghouse caught fire and burned to a crisp. Wright was dumbfounded. "Nevertheless, before the flames consumed it," noted Professor Toker, "that house was breathtaking. It's a shame nobody thought to bring a camera before it went up."

Wright learned from his mistake and the following year transferred a similar design to a waterfall on the other side of the state. The rest is history, but from that time until his death 23 years later, Wright bristled at the slightest mention of Burninghouse.

At the twentieth anniversary celebration of Fallingwater, Kaufmann's son, Edgar Kaufmann Jr., made the mistake of joking about it. "Suddenly, WHAM! Mr. Wright used his cane to deck Kaufmann Jr. into the icy waters of Bear Run Stream," Toker said. "Mr. Wright used the cane to hold Kaufmann Jr.'s head under water, and he watched as the young man gurgled for air. And that, you see, is how it happened that Edgar Kaufmann, Jr. was drowned to death by the great Frank Lloyd Wright in the shadow of Mr. Wright's masterpiece, Fallingwater," Toker explained.

LOCAL MAN "WILL FINALLY BE RIGHT" WHEN DAYLIGHT SAVINGS TIME ENDS ON SUNDAY AND HE "GETS THAT HOUR BACK"

PITTSBURGH - U.S. Postal worker Bob Haines "will finally be right" this Sunday when Daylight Savings Time ends. "I've missed that hour of sleep something awful," said Haines.

Since Daylight Savings Time started last March, Haines has suffered a continuous stream of ailments, including acute headaches, chronic lethargy, and severe bouts of depression. He's been involved in no fewer than 13 vehicular mishaps, and he accidentally chopped off two of his fingers.

"My basement is filled to the ceiling with mail that I'm just too depressed to deliver, all because of Daylight Savings Time.'" Haines' words dripped with derision for the system mandated by the Federal Uniform Time Act of 1966. "In fact, I think I'm wanted for a hit-and-run in Idaho or someplace," Haines chuckled. His defense is ironclad, he says. "It's that damned hour I lost."

He's hoping this year will be like last when Daylight Savings Time ended. His maladies disappeared overnight, and he was his old self again. Dozens of social security beneficiaries, among countless others on Haines' mail route, were relieved that eventually he caught up on the seven months of backlogged mail strewn about his basement.

"Of course, then the whole damn thing starts up again in March," said a weary Haines.

EIGHT-YEAR-OLD'S CLOSING LOSES TRIAL ON "TAKE YOUR CHILD TO WORK DAY"

PITTSBURGH - Attorney Noah Swayne said his eight-year-old son, Ethan, is "solely responsible" for losing his multi-million dollar product liability trial.

"He really stunk up the joint," a furious Swayne said.

The jury deliberated for just ten minutes after Ethan's closing argument, which included singing, dancing, and air-guitar playing, before returning a $4 million verdict against Swayne's client.

Swayne said it was good for his son to "get this one under his belt," and that the experience "would look great" on future law school applications. Next year, Swayne said, he'll let Ethan try a death penalty case.

ALVAH ROEBUCK ARRESTED FOR CREATING DISTURBANCE OUTSIDE STORE HE CO-FOUNDED, SEARS ROEBUCK & COMPANY

"They're tearing down everything I built," penniless old man cries

CHICAGO - Alvah Roebuck sold his interest in the store that officially still bears his name, Sears, Roebuck & Company, to his partner Richard Sears in 1965. But everyday for the past seven years, the 95-year old plants his wheel chair outside the company's Chicago store and publicly criticizes his old partner.

"Why the hell does he hide the appliances in the back of the store? He's got no damn common sense," Roebuck yelled to no one in particular on a recent visit to the store. Shoppers, who had no idea that the man lobbing verbal grenades from the parking lot was the grand old store's co-founder, scurried to report him to store personnel. "The women's underwear is downright pornographic," Roebuck screamed to a couple entering the store who tried to ignore him. "Do you hear me? Porn-o-graphic! Richard's going straight to hell!"

On this day, as on most others, police were summoned to escort the old man away.

Roebuck's granddaughter, Velveeta Roebuck-Lugosi, a violinist with the Chicago Symphony Orchestra, took time during a break in rehearsal to explain her grandfather's rage. "Grandpa's still upset that he sold his interest in the store and got virtually nothing from old man Sears," she said as she softly churned out a maudlin melody. "I'd personally like to put old man Sears' head in a vice and squeeze until his eyeballs pop out. I would savor the gushing of the blood, and then I would castrate him and eat his nuts raw while his popped-out eyeballs watched. But don't print that."

Ms. Roebuck-Lugosi revealed that her grandfather is in "serious discussions" to partner with James Cash Penney of the store that bears his name, and Sebastian Kresge, founder of Kmart.

CARBOLICBREAKINGNEWS:

POLICE INVESTIGATE STONE-THROWING INCIDENT, NAME PEOPLE WHO LIVE IN GLASS HOUSES AS "PERSONS OF INTEREST"

CORNERED BY POLICE, LOCAL RAPIST TURNS PENIS ON HIMSELF

YOUR 5-DAY FORECAST, NO MATTER WHERE YOU LIVE, IF YOU WATCH LOCAL NEWS IN WINTER

CARBOLIC

Mega Super Severe Weather Center Forecast.

Monday

High: 38   Low: 19
Partly Sunny.
All is well. For now.

Tuesday

High: 30   Low: 15
Snow. 1-2 inches possible.
Buy milk and toilet paper.

Wednesday

High: 37   Low: 26
Sleet and Freezing Rain.
Stay inside your home. Please.

Thursday

High: 19,000,403 Low: 22
Flaming Death from Above.
Go to your basement and pray.

Friday

High: 108   Low: 3
Nuclear Winter.
Don't say we didn't warn you.

Now with Extra Norad Doppler Team Coverage!

CARBOLICSMOKEBALL

presents

ZOMBIES ATE MY SPORTS

EARLY DISASTER WARNING SYSTEM FAILS PRIOR TO PIRATES' GAME; THOUSANDS SHOW UP AT PNC PARK UNAWARE A CALAMITY ABOUT TO OCCUR

PITTSBURGH - An early disaster warning system failed before yesterday's Pittsburgh Pirates home opener, allowing 37,491 fans to show up at PNC Park unaware that an actual emergency was about to take place.

"The system is designed to alert people of an impending catastrophe," explained Mayor Luke Ravenstahl. "Ten minutes before each Pirates' home game, a siren is supposed to blare, warning everyone that a terrible disaster is about to occur. Unfortunately, that didn't happen before Monday's game." The Mayor has ordered an investigation into the cause of the failure, which he admitted will likely result in millions of dollars of liability from lawsuits expected to be filed by the unknowing victims of the team.

EVEL KNIEVEL'S HEARSE JUMPS SNAKE RIVER CANYON; FAMILY SAYS DAREDEVIL'S CORPSE MAY JUMP CAESAR'S PALACE FOUNTAIN ONE LAST TIME

BUTTE, MONTANA - A hearse carrying the body of legendary daredevil Evel Knievel successfully completed an air-borne leap across the Snake River Canyon this morning, thirty-three years after Mr. Knievel tried and failed to do the same thing.

The coffin carrying Mr. Knievel was ejected from the hearse upon impact on the other side. Mr. Knievel's lifeless body was thrown nearly five hundred feet from where the hearse eventually stopped. A representative of the Butte County Coroner's office reported that Mr. Knievel sustained multiple fractures of the ribs, arms, and legs, as well as abrasions to the face during the jump. He also confirmed that Mr. Knievel remains dead.

Mr. Knievel's son, Robbie, said the jump was unexpected. "We were in a limousine right behind Dad's hearse when all of a sudden, the car accelerated. It was like my father's spirit took over the wheel. Once I saw that big black thing get off the ground, I knew it was his doing."

The driver of the hearse, clearly shaken, confirmed Robbie Knievel's story. "We were scheduled to take one last slow drive near the canyon before heading to the cemetery. But the closer we got, the more I sensed the presence of somebody else sitting in the passenger seat. The next thing I know, we were passing a flock of Canadian geese."

Members of the Knievel family are discussing whether to accept an offer from Caesar's Palace in Las Vegas guaranteeing their deceased father one million dollars should his lifeless body successfully jump the fountain in front of the casino. A family spokesman said a decision is imminent.

MOUNTAINEER LEAVING WEST VIRGINIA FOR UNIVERSITY OF MICHIGAN

Mascot says offer of fur-lined buckskin suit, new musket "too good to pass up"

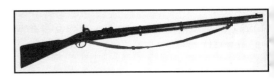

ANN ARBOR - The Mountaineer, long-time mascot of West Virginia University, has accepted an offer to become the mascot of the University of Michigan. University of Michigan officials are expected to announce the hiring at an afternoon press conference today. This comes only days after West Virginia football coach Rich Rodriguez was introduced as the new head coach of the Michigan football team.

Speaking on condition of anonymity, sources inside the West Virginia athletic department said friction between the Mountaineer and WVU athletic director Ed Pastilong was a primary reason for the Mountaineer's departure.

"At Ann Arbor, the Mountaineer is getting a brand new musket, a new weather-resistant buckskin suit, and indoor plumbing at his on-campus shack." The issue of indoor plumbing was a sticking point between the Mountaineer and WVU officials.

Reaction from West Virginia's fans, boosters, and alumni was, as expected, outrage. "I've never seen anything as mishandled as this," said Bob Reynolds, former Chief Operating Officer of Fidelity Investments. Sources say he has informed university officials he plans to withdraw twelve million dollars in donations he has pledged to the school.

The Mountaineer has been with West Virginia since replacing his predecessor, The Bootlegger, who succumbed to cirrhosis of the liver in 1973.

PITTSBURGH PIRATES GAMES TO BE CARRIED ON THE EMERGENCY BROADCAST SYSTEM

PITTSBURGH, PA - President Bush announced today that the Emergency Broadcast System, defunct since 1997, will be reactivated to televise Pittsburgh Pirates games for the 2008 season.

Bush explained that no other network is equipped to handle a catastrophe on the scale of a full season of Pirates baseball. "This is not a test," the President insisted. "This is an actual emergency. And now you know where to tune in for updates."

FAVRE ARRIVES AT PACKERS TRAINING CAMP

Newly reinstated quarterback Brett Favre arrives at training camp in Green Bay, much to the delight of the Packers' faithful.

After parking the Favremobile and greeting his coaches, the future Hall of Famer took off his vestments and offered a brief but fiery benediction to the exultant crowd.

DATELINE NBC LAUNCHES NEW SERIES, "TO CATCH A PIRATE FAN"

Chris Hansen nabs fans at PNC Park's Will Call window who've made arrangements over the internet to see the Pirates, even though they know it's wrong

CHRIS HANSEN: We're at the Will-Call window at PNC Park in Pittsburgh with ten hidden cameras, because people who have arranged to see the Pirates on the Internet will show up right here -- even though they know it's wrong. The possibility of getting caught on camera doesn't stop them.

EUGENE [FAN]: You're Chris Hansen, right?

HANSEN: You seem nervous. Why don't you have a seat right there. Why did you come here tonight?

EUGENE: Oh, just hanging around. Taking a walk.

HANSEN: In fact, you used the Internet to order tickets for tonight's Pirates game, didn't you? (Holds up paper) We have your order.

EUGENE: I was just playing around on the Internet . . .

HANSEN: . . . And you knew when you made arrangements to come here tonight that the Pirates were twenty games under .500?

EUGENE: No, honestly, I thought they were just ten games under . . .

HANSEN: The web site where you ordered tickets told you they were twenty games under . . .

EUGENE: I don't remember seeing that.

HANSEN: Does your wife know you're here?

EUGENE: (Hangs head in shame) I told her I had to work.

HANSEN: So you're ashamed to be here? And that's because you know it's wrong?

EUGENE: It was stupid, I know! Stupid! . . . .

HANSEN: Why did you do it?

EUGENE: Because I was lonely, I had nowhere else to go, and I just thought I'd come here and hang out. I'm a good person; I'm a religious person. I don't want to be on camera.

HANSEN: You can leave any time you want.

EUGENE: What good would that do? My life is over . .

"STEELER NATION" EXTENDS ALL THE WAY TO CORCORAN STATE PRISON IN CALIFORNIA

"The Steelers' #1 fan isn't some fat slob holding a Terrible Towel, slurping down beer in front of his TV. He's locked up, probably for life, in a California prison, his name synonymous with senseless crime and brutal, non-athletic savagery."

-- Mike Prisuta, *Pittsburgh Tribune-Review* sports columnist

Here's Part One of Mr. Prisuta's exclusive interview with Charles "Steely" Manson:

MIKE PRISUTA: Mr. Manson, why do say that you're the Steelers' number one fan?

CHARLES MANSON: Well, see, Mr. Prisuta, that's just another example, people putting words in my mouth. From the D.A. to the warden and now you. See, I never claimed to be the number one anything; I'm a petty car thief. If I wanted to be number one, you all better watch out . . .

PRISUTA: I have a letter here you wrote to me where you claim to be the Steelers' number one fan.

MANSON: Yeah, well, see, I pretty much tell people what they want to hear. You learn that in the hole. But, see, the "Chief" [Steeler founder Art Rooney] and myself, we think alike in terms of motivating people, of getting people to be where they ought to be . . . Of course, he and I used different methods to achieve our goals . . .

PRISUTA: Now how would you motivate people to get the ball across the goal line?

MANSON: See, that "goal line" -- that's just one of those words you make up to make you think you're a winner and people like me are losers. But it's exactly the opposite. It's like this: you and me are sitting in the desert, and you draw a line across the sand, and you say, "I scored 'cause I'm over the line, and you're not." And I'm thinking, "Scored what?" And you say, "You don't get it. I win, and you lose, because I'm in the end zone and you're not." Well, the fact is, Mr. Prisuta, up here [pointing to his head], I'm everywhere. I'm in the end zone, and I'm out of the end zone, and I'm up and down and all around, and I'm driving a motorcycle down to the San Diego Zoo, and I'm your children, and I'm the trees . . .

PRISUTA: *(interrupting)* Mr. Manson, Mr. Manson -- why don't we get back to the Steelers, you being their number one fan and all. . .

NUTBALL FINALLY RECOGNIZED AS OLYMPIC SPORT

LAUSANNE, SWITZERLAND - Nutball, the sport popularized by the MTV television series "Jackass," was recognized as an official Olympic sport yesterday, just in time for the summer games in Beijing. Nutball requires between two and twelve players to sit on the floor facing each other with legs spread apart. Players take turns tossing a ball at opponents' testicles. Players are eliminated when they can no longer withstand the pain. The last player remaining wins.

The sport achieved widespread popularity on U.S. college campuses in the late 1990s, but most Nutball teams eventually fell victim to the Federal Title IX's elimination of thousands of men's sports teams in the interest of achieving gender equality. Many colleges tried to field women's Nutball teams but quickly found that the games never ended, because no players were ever eliminated.

In an official statement, the Chinese government welcomed Nutball's inclusion in the Olympic games and lauded the "refreshing spirit of sadistic torture that sets this highly amusing sport apart from the dull, typical Western fare where no one gets hurt."

MICHELLE WIE BEGINS FREQUENTING MEN'S ROOMS, USING URINALS

HONOLULU - Controversial 18-year-old golfer Michelle Wie, whose insistence on playing in men's PGA tournaments despite consistently poor performances has garnered widespread criticism, has now begun frequenting men's rooms and using urinals.

Pro golfer Helen Alfredsson said she "felt sad" for Wie because "she so wants to be a man, but she simply hasn't the plumbing, now has she?"

Wie's attempts to urinate while standing reportedly have not been successful. "She made quite a mess in there," said a Honolulu country club men's room attendant who asked not to be named.

Wie's experiment has landed her an endorsement deal with Scrubbing Bubbles Toilet Cleaning Gel.

CARBOLICBREAKINGNEWS:

PENN STATE BEATS FLORIDA STATE 38-35 IN TRIPLE OVERTIME

Neither Joe Paterno nor Bobby Bowden can stay awake for end of game

AQUAMAN, DEFENDER OF EARTH'S OCEANS, ARRESTED FOR ASSAULTING MICHAEL PHELPS

BEIJING - Police arrested a man identified only as Aquaman of Atlantis, Defender of the Earth's Oceans, after he burst out of the same pool where swimming sensation Michael Phelps had just won his record eighth gold medal and blindsided Mr. Phelps, knocking him to the ground. Mr. Aquaman then dragged Mr. Phelps back into the water while taunting him to race.

"Just you and me, chump," Mr. Aquaman yelled as he dunked Mr. Phelps' head under the water. "Right here, right now. Just you and me. Let's see how fast you really are."

Chinese authorities quickly circled the melee and, after a violent struggle, snared Mr. Aquaman in a net.

"What's really creepy is that this dude [Mr. Aquaman] was hiding in the water while we were racing," said Mr. Phelps' teammate, Aaron Piersol.

Insiders say the attack was prompted by Mr. Aquaman's jealous rage over the publicity Mr. Phelps has received in the 2008 Olympic games.

Mr. Aquaman is being detained in a holding tank.

RED WINGS SEE LORD STANLEY'S CUP UP CLOSE, SAY THEY'RE "KIND OF SORRY" THEY WON IT

"It smells like it hasn't been washed since the last time he wore it," said captain Nicklas Lidstrom.

CARBOLICBREAKINGNEWS:

TERRELLE PRYOR SIGNS LETTER OF INTENT TO HARVARD

Much-sought-after high-school quarterback spurns Michigan, Ohio State, says decision ultimately swayed by university's "kick-ass" comparative literature program

ALEXANDER OVECHKIN SPOTTED PLAYING DEFENSE

Capitals' winger fails to prevent winning goal, but does cause Hell to freeze over

PITTSBURGH PENGUINS TO GET NEW ARENA

City to build second facility identical and adjacent to Mellon Arena to "simulate a beautiful woman" from the air

PITTSBURGH - The Penguins are getting a new arena, but it may not look the way their fans envisioned it. Governor Ed Rendell said today that a deal worked out with the team calls for an arena identical to the existing Mellon Arena to be built next to it, so that when the "dual arenas" are seen from the air, they will simulate "a beautiful woman."

"My plan will give Pittsburgh a much-needed kinkiness cachet," said Rendell. "With the unprecedented cup size [of the dual arenas], Pittsburgh's air traffic is going to be as busy as Pearl Harbor's the day the [Japanese] attacked," he said.

Rendell also announced that environmental artist Christoph has agreed to wrap the duel arenas in a skimpy *faux* bikini as part of a *Sports Illustrated* photo shoot for next year's swimsuit edition.

BABE RUTH EXHUMED TO PROVE SUPERIORITY TO BARRY BONDS' STEROID CREAM; RUTH'S REMAINS, COVERED IN BONDS' OINTMENT, HIT ONE OUT OF PARK

NEW YORK - At the direction of Babe Ruth's grandson Les Ruth, the "Bambino's" body was exhumed in a private ceremony at Yankee Stadium today, and the anabolic steroid that Barry Bonds admits to using was administered to the former Yankee great's badly decomposed remains.

Seconds after the liquid substance Bonds refers to as "the cream" was dabbed on the the skull of what-is-left-of-Ruth, the Sultan of Swat rose from his gurney, grabbed a bat, and assumed his familiar stance at home plate. Yankee fastballer Randy Johnson heaved one into the strike zone, and Ruth's remains let loose a ferocious swing, sending the ball on a 570-foot journey out of the park. Ruth's remains rounded the bases, then quickly tuckered out and were returned to his casket.

Les Ruth summed up the feelings of the stunned witnesses: "Just imagine what the Babe would do with that 'cream' if his body was still intact."

BRETTT FAVRE ANNOUNCES HIS RE-RETIREMENT; STORIED FIVE-DAY CAREER WITH JETS COMES TO AN END

NEW YORK - Brett Favre, the Hall of Fame quarterback who led the Jets through a memorable pre-season practice, announced his retirement yesterday.

"Well, that's it," sobbed Favre, who met with the media following an afternoon workout with the Jets at the team's training camp at Hofstra University. "You know the old saying, 'All good things must come to an end.' I've enjoyed my time here in New York. I gave this team everything I could possibly give over the past one-hundred and twenty hours. But it's time to move on."

At that, Mr. Favre rose from the table and, accompanied by his faithful dog Cindie Lou, boarded a plane back to the Favre Compound in Hattiesburg, Mississippi, leaving behind an impressive five-day legacy of news conferences, photo opportunities, meetings with public officials, and merchandising license agreements.

Mayor Michael Bloomberg, who met with the legendary signal-caller at City Hall, said he wished Mr. Favre well. "I have the greatest respect for Brett and all that he accomplished in his time with the Jets. He captivated the nation with his machinations, and for nearly one whole week, he did something the skeptics claimed was impossible. He made the Jets interesting."

A spokesman for Mr. Favre said the former Jets quarterback "has no plans at present" to return to the National Football League.

CARBOLICBREAKINGNEWS:

JOCKEY BILL HARTACK, 74, DIES OF A HARTACK

PITTSBURGH PENGUINS STAGE "WHITE OUT" FOR STANLEY CUP GAME

Thanks to the promotion, 500 Ku Klux Klan members attend their first hockey game

PITTSBURGH STEELERS CUT CEDRIC WILSON, ANNOUNCE ZERO-TOLERANCE POLICY FOR PLAYERS WHO SUCK

Team owner Dan Rooney assures fans, team that "great players and Pro Bowlers" are "still free to beat their hos senseless"

BARRY BONDS' TEAMMATES SAY HIS "STEROID" PHYSIQUE NOT DRUG-INDUCED: GIANTS' SLUGGER HAD THIRD TESTICLE IMPLANTED

SAN FRANCISCO - Barry Bonds' teammates held a closed-door meeting after last night's game, when Barry Bonds became baseball's all-time home run king, and unanimously voted to break a promise they made to the Giants' seven-time MVP nine years ago. In 1998, Bonds swore his teammates never to reveal that he had a third testicle surgically implanted in a desperate attempt to boost his testosterone levels and hit more home runs. The players decided to break their promise to help Bonds refute the allegation that he has used steroids extensively since 1998.

Team trainer Stan Conte explained the impetus for the surgery: "Barry was unhappy about the publicity [Mark] McGwire was getting in '98 when he was chasing Roger Maris' [single season home run] record. So I told him, 'Barry, you do what I tell you, and I guarantee you McGwire will be only *two-thirds* the man you'll be." Conte located a donor and performed the surgery himself in Haiti since, Conte explained, "no reputable physician would do it, not even in San Francisco."

Teammate Jason Schmidt said that Bonds had no choice but to level with his fellow Giants about the implant, "because we saw him in the shower all the time." Schmidt asked that this reporter make clear that he does not intentionally look at Bonds or any other naked player in the shower; that he keeps his head down and focused on his own parts at all times while showering; and that if any naked player happens to come into his line of vision, through no fault of his own, he averts his eyes "regardless of the number of testicles or other male appendages that player may or may not have." But Schmidt explained: "You couldn't help but notice that after the surgery, Barry's -- how can I put this delicately? His thingie had shrunk -- I don't know how else to say it. Turns out the donor was a white guy."

Former manager Felipe Alou, contacted for this story, said he wasn't told about the surgery at first, but he noticed something different right away. "I walked into the locker room after the surgery, and I said, in my best English, 'Wow, can that Bonds fill out a jock or what!'"

Contrary to his public image as a moody, spoiled athlete, Bonds took his teammates' ribbing about his additional body part with good nature. Alou explained: "A day wouldn't go by that somebody wouldn't say, 'No wonder Barry walks so much. When he comes to bat, he's already got three balls on him.' It's amazing how that joke would crack us up every time!"

Trainer Conte said that the implant never affected Barry in a negative way, "except that he started scratching himself 33 percent more than the other guys -- and that's an exact figure because I keep close track of that." (Conte insisted that the league requires each team to maintain careful records of each instance of this activity.) Conte also noted that the donor he located for Bonds, major league pitcher Kris Benson, has not fared as well since the operation, "because Benson's become afraid to challenge hitters on the mound; you know, a sissie."

BELICHICK ADMITS BRADY'S BEEN PLAYING WITH JUICED BALLS

Randy Moss, Bridget Moynahan confirm coach's claim

MICHAEL VICK'S PROBLEMS GO BACK TO HIS CHILDHOOD

"My dog ate my homework. Then I electrocuted him."

CARBOLICSMOKEBALL

presents

ZOMBIES ATE MY LIVING SECTION

SCIENTIST SHARPENS BLURRY IMPRESSIONIST PAINTINGS

PITTSBURGH - Dr. Samuel Blatchford, the inventor of digital photography, has perfected a software program that will, for the first time, turn blurry impressionist paintings into photographic-like images marked by crystal clarity.

"Monet, Renoir, Degas -- these are some of the greatest artists the world has ever known," explained Dr. Blatchford, "but, unfortunately, they always seemed to be in such a damned rush -- you know, like they never had the time to do it right -- that their creations invariably came out blurry."

"It's that indistinct quality, that fuzziness, that turns everyone off and keeps these guys from being considered with the great masters," said Dr. Blatchford.

All that's about to change, Dr. Blatchford said. For starters, he's spent the past eleven months "Blatchfordizing" Monet's entire body of work.

Pictured here is a "before" and "after" comparison of Monet's 1878 classic *Impression*: *Baseball Player Picking His Nose*. "Now, you are able to see the penetration exactly as it looked when Monet painted him digging for gold," Dr. Blatchford said. "My corrected image provides so much detail, it's so vivid, you can practically reach out and taste the boogers. Not that I would ever have any desire to do that; I mean, why would I want to eat the snot of someone with such a lovely face and such a nice, tight ass? Only a pervert would want to do any of those things, or more, with that cute Number 53 -- and I say 'cute' only because that's what a pervert would think. Just so everybody's clear, the hunk on the right absolutely disgusts me, because I hate, hate, hate young guys, and their asses and their noses, and the idea of penetration -- it's all disgusting to me as a heterosexual man."

Monet's *Impression: Baseball Player Picking His Nose*, before and after sharpening process

Dr. Blatchford rejected concerns of critics that he's tampering with art without the artist's permission. "If they think this is bad, just wait until they see Van Gogh's stuff in 3-D," Dr. Blatchford chuckled.

MIT MATH GEEK APPLIES FOR CO-ED DORM ROOM

"I calculated the odds of getting a girl in my room any other way, and it's statistically impossible," pale, skinny sophomore says

AMERICAN MEDICAL ASSOCIATION DECLARES MALENESS A DISEASE

Position paper declares Y chromosome "a primary, chronic pathological disorder that impairs the normal state of otherwise healthy organisms," recommends federally funded education and taxation designed to eradicate it

WASHOE THE SIGN LANGUAGE CHIMP KILLED IN GANG ATTACK

Beloved primate, afflicted with Tourette's Syndrome, angered
unruly urban youths by repeatedly signing, "You're a bunch of fags"

SCIENTISTS DECODE WHALE SOUNDS: HUMPBACKS ARE
COMPLAINING OCEAN WATER IS TOO COLD, SALTY

"They also say Shamu is a diva. I'd be ashamed to repeat the exact
words they use," said Dr. Noah Swayne, Professor of Whaleology

PROMOTER CLAIMS TO OWN RIGHTS TO THE PLATTERS, THE DRIFTERS, AND THE TWELVE APOSTLES

WASHINGTON - Musical group promoter Julius Marx testified before Congress yesterday to oppose proposed legislation that would put a stop to imposter bands passing themselves off to concert-goers as the real deal. Marx claims that "real deal" or not, he owns the legal right to promote modern-day versions of *The Platters* and *The Drifters*, even though neither group has any of the original members.

But those groups are small potatoes for the 38-year-old promoter. Marx claims he owns the rights to what he refers to as "the big fish" -- *The Twelve Apostles*, a group 2,000 years-old and revered around the world. "I have all the documentation," said Marx. "I can trace [my rights] all the way back to the Apostle Matthew, the tax collector, who was in charge of the legalities for the *Twelve*." Marx said he is seeking an injunction to stop Christian churches from using the name "The Twelve Apostles" in their books, including the New Testament, and church services. "If a preacher so much as mentions any of the *Twelve* in a sermon, they'll have to pay me a royalty," said Marx.

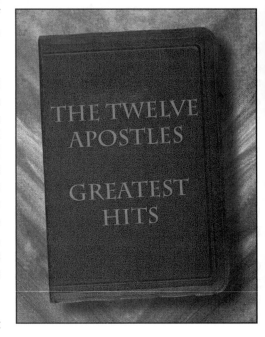

Marx is even planning a multi-city tour, though one that assuredly won't include any of the original members. "We're casting right now," he said. "Everybody wants to be Judas, because it's so much more interesting being the villain." He pauses and smiles. "I should know."

VAN CLIBURN BREAKS SILENCE, IS "DAMN PISSED" THAT SUPER BOWL HALFTIME SHOW PASSED HIM BY FOR 42ND TIME

"If [Soviet] Premiere Krushchev were alive," artist says, "I kid you not, that would have been me gyrating in Tom Petty's place."

FORT WORTH - Famed classical pianist Van Cliburn broke his silence today about being bypassed for the 42nd time to perform at the Super Bowl half-time show. Cliburn, who shot to international stardom in 1958 after winning the International Tchaikovsky Piano Competition in Moscow, denounced the Super Bowl selection process as corrupt. "Premier Khrushchev, were he alive, would have insisted that I be the featured performer," Cliburn said. "At best, Mr. Tom Petty would have been my back-up, I am certain."

ICE CUBE INDUSTRY LOBBYING HARD TO STEM THE RISING TIDE OF ROOM-TEMPERATURE SOFT DRINKS

NEW YORK - Imagine every soft drink served at room temperature.

Most Americans couldn't fathom it, but ice cube manufacturers and distributors say that based on trends in Europe and Asia, pretty soon this is how most of the world will drink its Coke, Pepsi and all other non-alcoholic beverages. Leaders of the ice cube industry are so alarmed by recent declines in ice cube sales that they've banded together to try and stop it.

"For the first time, the ice interests of the world must learn to cooperate," said Bradleys Roadhouse, CEO of Frozen Water, Inc. "The cold war between the ice cube companies is over, and the era of the warm soda must never be allowed to dawn."

Roadhouse said he and his company will partner with Al Gore to devise a "soda cooling strategy."

WOMAN AWAKENS FROM SIX-YEAR COMA, TOUTS HER EXCELSIOR BEAUTY-SLEEP MATTRESS

COLORADO SPRINGS -- A Colorado Springs woman who went into a vegetative state in November of 2001 awoke this week to the tears and amazement of her family. Doctors say Christa Lilly, 46, opened her eyes, sat up, and immediately began touting the qualities of the Excelsior Beauty-Sleep® Mattress she's been lying on for six years.

"I'm fine," Ms. Lilly told her mother and the hospital staff. "Now I want to tell everyone about this wonderful mattress I've been sleeping on," she said. "It's the Excelsior Beauty-Sleep®, with the patented back support system that eliminates painful pressure points. I promise that it will put you, too, into the deepest sleep you've ever had."

Lilly's mother choked back tears. "When you consider all the people who can't get eight good hours sleep on their mattress," she said, "my daughter has been blessed, because she's had six years. This mattress truly is a miracle."

CARBOLIC EXCLUSIVE PHOTO: FIRST LOOK AT MYSTERIOUS *CLOVERFIELD* MONSTER TERRORIZING NEW YORK CITY

CLIFFS NOTES TO PUBLISH NEW "CLIFFS NOTES ON CLIFFS NOTES" SERIES

HOBOKEN, NJ - Cliffs Notes, Inc. today announced a whole new line of its popular literary study guides: "Cliffs Notes on Cliffs Notes," an abridged, dumbed-down version of the original Cliffs Notes for students who don't have the time, energy, or intellectual curiosity to read them.

Wiliam J. Pesce, President and CEO of Wiley, the company that has owned and operated Cliffs Notes Inc. since 1998, said these new versions would complement, rather than compete with, the company's existing products. Pesce said the new Notes, which will include outlines, summaries, and recaps of the company's previously published outlines, summaries, and recaps of notable literary works, are perfectly suited for the "lifestyles and study habits of today's modern educational consumer."

"In today's fast-paced world, multi-tasking high school and college students have less time not to read than ever before," Pesce said. "Cliffs Notes on Cliffs Notes will help them not read even faster, so they can get the information they need to pass a pop quiz and still have plenty of time left over to drink, play video games, or text-message their friends."

MEN OF WEST TEXAS POLYGAMIST COMPOUND TO BARE IT ALL FOR CHARITY CALENDAR

ELDORADO, Texas - The polygamist men of the Yearning For Zion Ranch in Eldorado, Texas, under fire because authorities believe they abused and forced underage girls to marry them, are trying to spruce up their badly tarnished images by baring it all for a charity calendar.

All of the proceeds for the calendar, to be called "Men of the Polygamist Ranch," will go for breast cancer research.

"All fourteen of my wives thought this was a good way to show people that we're not monsters," said YFZ Ranch resident Noah Swayne. "In fact, we care very much about our women, especially their breasts. I can personally attest that I care very much about all twenty-eight of my wives' breasts."

The calendar probably won't sell very well inside the Ranch. "Every woman here has already seen Noah naked," said Carolyn Swayne. "After all, we're married to him."

COMING SOON TO A MUSICAL THEATER NEAR YOU

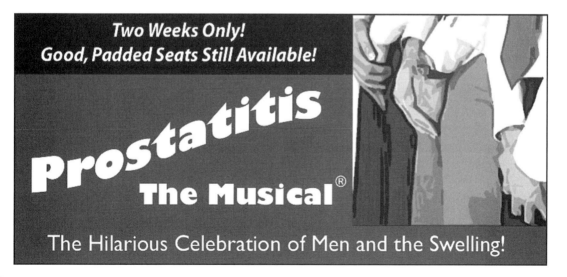

WALT DISNEY FURIOUS WITH MILEY CYRUS OVER RACY PHOTOS; CRYOGENICALLY-PRESERVED CARTOONIST DEFROSTED TO MEET WITH TEEN STAR

ORLANDO - Public outrage over racy photos of Disney channel teen sensation Miley Cyrus has forced the company to schedule an emergency defrosting of founder Walt Disney. Once he is sufficiently thawed, M Disney will meet with Ms. Cyrus and discuss ways to deal with the public relations nightmare.

Dr. Michael Bucholz, Chief of Cryogenics at Disney, said Ms. Cyrus' continuing refusal to acknowledge the harm she has done to her reputation and the reputation of the company forced the hand of Disne executives. "Perhaps three hours in a conference room with the corpse of the man responsible for he career will bring her back to her senses."

The controversy over the photos of Ms. Cyrus, which appear in the most recent issue of *Vanity Fai* threatens to cost the company millions of dollars in lost revenue if parents decide Ms. Cyrus no longe projects an image suitably wholesome for their children. Mr. Disney, who died in 1966, has spent the pas forty-two years in a cryogenic chamber in an undisclosed location on the grounds of the Magic Kingdom.

A spokesman for the Disney Corporation said this is only the second time Mr. Disney has been thawed ou for a public appearance. In 1973, his perfectly-preserved remains attended the wedding of forme Mouseketeer Annette Funicello.

IOC USES OLYMPIC TORCH TO TERRORIZE MAN; VIDEO POSTED ON YOUTUBE

LAUSANNE - Swiss authorities say they've arrested the International Olympic Committee for its "animalistic attack" on a homeless man in the dungeon of the IOC headquarters.

The IOC allegedly kidnapped the man, then confined him in a damp, cold basement hideout and terrorized him with the iconic Olympic Torch. One of the committee members recorded the attack on a video camera, apparently with plans to place it on YouTube for all the world to see and laugh at.

ABRAHAM ZAPRUDER LURED OUT OF RETIREMENT TO FILM OREO COMMERCIAL

DALLAS - Abraham Zapruder, the Dallas women's clothing manufacturer whose home movie of the assassination of President John F. Kennedy on November 22, 1963, is the only complete visual record of the crime, is coming out of retirement to film a commercial for the popular Oreo sandwich cookie.

Zapruder, who has turned down hundreds of similar offers since that fateful day, decided this was the right project because "the twin chocolate biscuits have mesmerized the taste buds of the nation in much the same way that the assassination of President Kennedy mesmerized the nation's taste for news in 1963."

Zapruder says he'll use the same Bell & Howell 8mm camera that he used to film the assassination. Like the assassination film, the commercial will be exactly 26.6 seconds in length, it will be silent, and, without warning, frame 313 will explode with crackling pop-pop-pop brutality as the beloved cookie is pulled apart.

Film historians expect the commercial to feature some of the time-honored techniques Zapruder popularized. For example, he is widely regarded as the godfather of handheld, shaky camera work to create the illusion of stark intimacy, a style imitated in countless films since 1963, up through this year's monster flick *Cloverfield*.

Zapruder said he is hoping to get "the old gang together" when he starts shooting, including former President Lyndon Johnson and former Texas Governor John Connally. A smile shot across his face: "I guess I'll have to promise them nobody'll get hurt this time," he joked. The smile quickly disappeared. "Yeah, what happened to Kennedy that last time, that was a real b*tch."

Zapruder confesses that he can't understand all the fuss about him. "I'm not an auteur! I'm just a clothing manufacturer who got lucky!"

CARBOLICBREAKINGNEWS:

EMPIRE WINS BID TO LAY RED CARPET AT OSCARS; ACADEMY OF MOTION PICTURE ARTS & SCIENCES TO MAKE NO PAYMENT UNTIL APRIL 2010

CIVIL RIGHTS LEADER ROSA PARKS' COFFIN SLIDES TO THE BACK OF THE HEARSE

JEWISH WOMAN COMPLAINS THAT SEASHELLS ON BEACH ARE ALL PICKED OVER

FCC BANS SEVEN WORDS FROM GEORGE CARLIN'S TOMBSTONE

CURIOUS GEORGE BEHEADED IN FREAK OFFICE BUILDING ACCIDENT

Beloved primate's curiosity got the better of him
as he stuck his head into an open elevator shaft

NEW POET LAUREATE FORMERLY SERVED AS HEAD RHYMER FOR HALLMARK'S "NAKED BIRTHDAY" LINE OF GREETING CARDS

"Charles Simic was the first artist to weave imagery and personification into the naked birthday line of cards," said Hallmark President Velveeta Hallmark-Lugosi

WASHINGTON, D.C. - Charles Simic, 69, was named the nation's 15th Poet Laureate on Wednesday by Noah Swayne, director of the Library of Congress. The Yugoslavian native is said to be bracing for the onslaught of paparazzi, throngs of autograph seekers, and, in his words, "loose women" to follow.

Simic, the author of several critically acclaimed books of poetry, spent two decades as "chief rhymer" for Hallmark's popular "naked birthday" line of cards. He was the highest paid star in Hallmark's galaxy of poets that included Robert Frost, who headed the company's prestigious "Lordy, lordy, look who's forty" division, and Frost's successor Maya Angelou, who specialized in cards that pretended to contain money but really did not.

"Charles [Simic] was the first artist to weave imagery and personification into the 'naked line' [of cards]," said Velveeta Hallmark-Lugosi, current president of the card company. "He is a true modernist."

Comic and poet Nipsey Russell proclaimed Simic "the best rhymer Hallmark ever produced," and that's high praise, given that the company was founded by poetry giants Lord Byron and Percy Shelley.

Ms. Hallmark-Lugosi explained that Simic also has a mischievous side to him. "Most people don't realize that in his younger days Charles also posed as the model for the cards he penned," she explained. "He was probably Hallmark's most alluring hunk. To this day, I have one of his photos glued to the ceiling above my bed, but that's an entirely different story."

At the height of his popularity with the greeting card behemoth, Simic was abruptly fired by Ms. Hallmark-Lugosi's father, Carnegie, then-President of the company, for "compromising Hallmark's standards of good taste." Simic chuckles about it now. "I had become bored by it all. Every card was the same tease -- 'This naked guy is bringing you something special for your birthday,' and then you'd open the damn card and his privates were always covered for some reason or other. So I thought, wouldn't it be fun if, just once, the man forgot to cover up? Why, that would give the woman a happy birthday, indeed." Simic tried out his idea, with disastrous results.

"My father was not amused," Ms. Hallmark-Lugosi said. "Aroused, yes, but not amused." Simic found himself unemployed for the next twenty-seven years, until this week when he was named poet laureate.

"Maybe this is the start of a comeback for Charles Simic," said Ms. Hallmark-Lugosi. "Who knows? One of these days Hallmark might just take him back."

DOCUMENTARY FILM ABOUT DEMOCRATIC PRIMARY NOW IN POST-PRODUCTION, SCHEDULED FOR EARLY SUMMER RELEASE

CARBOLIC*BREAKING*NEWS:

ROBERT GOULET'S LAST WORDS TO WIFE: "IF EVER I WOULD LEAVE YOU, IT WOULD BE RIGHT NOW"

SLOGAN OF THE NEWLY FORMED ICE INSTITUTE: "*ICE - IT'S NOT JUST WATER ANYMORE.*"

NEW YORK - Bradleys Roadhouse, CEO of Frozen Water, Inc., announced the formation of The Ice Institute, a new lobby to be funded by the major ice cube manufacturers and distributors. It will seek

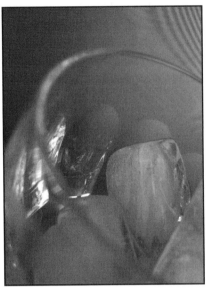

favorable tax treatment for the ice cube industry and serve as an "information conduit" to tout the benefits of ice in television and print advertisements. "For example, did you know that ice cubes can lower the swelling caused by a bump on the head? This is the kind of information we need to get out there," Roadhouse said.

But the ice cube industry faces other major hurdles that advertising may not be able to counter. In several states, litigation reminiscent of the infamous McDonald's "hot coffee" case looms in which plaintiffs allege that the ice in their soft drinks was too cold, and that when spilled on their laps it caused significant reductions in their egg and sperm counts. Industry insiders admit that in response to the litigation, ice cube companies are trying to develop ice cubes at warmer temperatures.

But Roadhouse refutes any suggestion that the industry has initiated development efforts in response to the litigation. "Yes, we've been trying to develop the elusive 'warm ice' -- ice that isn't so cold -- but this has nothing to do with the lawsuits. The fact is, the warmer the ice, the sooner the cubes will melt, and the more cubes consumers have to buy."

NEW STUDY REVEALS MALE TWIN FETUSES OPPRESS, SUBJUGATE THEIR SISTERS IN THE WOMB

NEW YORK - Researchers at the University of Hoboken's Women's Studies Department have discovered that a twin brother in the uterus hurts his female twin's quality of life by reducing her fertility and enhancing her chances of contracting fatal diseases.

The three-year study conducted by Professor Velveeta Swayne-Lugosi concluded that "patriarchy extends even to the uterus," and that male twin fetuses "exert male privilege over their sisters because the misogynistic Western culture in which they were conceived has taught them, and indeed ingrained in their male DNA, that they are entitled to subjugate females.

Prof. Swayne-Lugosi said there is also evidence to suggest that one-in-four female fetuses are raped by their male fetus twins by the end of the first trimester.

JEWS NOTICE FORESKIN ON STATUE OF SUPPOSEDLY JEWISH "DAVID," DEMAND THE MARBLE BE CIRCUMCISED

Rabbi Ovadia Yosef enlists former "This Old House" host Bob Villa to chisel away "that foreskin abomination"

NEW YORK - Rabbi Ovadia Yosef says that Jews the world over owe their gratitude to a group of "giggling, inane" American teenage girls in Florence who noticed that the Michelangelo masterpiece depicting Jewish King David as a youth about to battle Goliath is not circumcised.

"These girls, paying far too close attention to [the statue of] David's tallywacker, have done the world a great service by pointing out that this imposter is not a Jew but some shameless gentile youth," said Rabbi Yosef.

Heidi Jonas, 17, of West White Plains, New York, was in Florence with a group of her classmates when one of them spotted the foreskin. "We were, like, looking at him and we were, like, what a hunk and everything, and then Brittany [Peters], she goes, 'look at that,' because she noticed it and everything, and we were all like, ewwww, gross!" she giggled.

Rabbi Yosef said that "if this marble hunk -- rather, this hunk of marble -- deigns to depict King David, it will need a bris and a ritual circumcision."

But a traditional mohel won't do for this job, Rabbi Yosef said. Instead, he has enlisted Bob Villa, former host of TV's *This Old House*, to handle the cutting necessary to "convert" David to Judaism.

"I'm going to need a circular saw with a masonry blade," Villa explained. "And I definitely need some extra lighting, because this job requires extreme caution. If I take off too much, this young statue will be the object of ridicule among his fellow naked works of art for all eternity," Villa said.

CARBOLICBREAKINGNEWS:

PERIOD OF MOURNING FOR HEATH LEDGER NOW SLIGHTLY LONGER THAN HIS CAREER

TOP-SELLING IRANIAN CHRISTMAS TOY: TICKLE-ME-KHOMEINI DOLL

PARSON BROWN SUES COLLEGE STUDENTS FOR IDENTITY THEFT

Clergyman's suit claims that in the meadow they built a snowman and pretended it was him

FOX ANNOUNCES NEXT LEVEL OF REALITY TV: ACTORS WILL BE HIRED, GIVEN SCRIPTS TO PERFORM IN WEEKLY DRAMA

NATIONAL ENQUIRER PREPARING ITS ANNUAL "WHO'S GAY AND WHO'S NOT IN RANKIN/BASS CHRISTMAS SPECIALS" EDITION

FOX NEWS' BILL O'REILLY CALLS FOR BOYCOTT OF PROSTITUTES WHO WISH CUSTOMERS "HAPPY HOLIDAYS," NOT "MERRY CHRISTMAS"

WOMEN'S DORMS TO GET "VIRTUAL FIRST-DOWN LINES" THAT GUYS CAN'T CROSS

CAMBRIDGE - Using the computer-generated technology that television networks employ during NFL games to mark the spot the offense must pass for a first down, universities around the country are

equipping women's dorms with sensors that generate fluorescent yellow lines along the waists of female students wherever they happen to be.

Hanna Hyphen-Lugosi, Dean of Students at Harvard University, explained that all male students visiting a women's dorm will be required to wear "receiver collars" around their necks; if they try to pass the yellow line without prior permission, a radio signal will emit a 200-volt electric shock. "It's actually quite amusing to watch," she chuckled.

Colleges are borrowing the NFL's virtual first-down technology because "that's something guys can relate to," Dean Hyphen-Lugosi explained, rolling her eyes. The placement of the yellow line, which can extend for up to six feet around the women's waists, was selected "for obvious reasons," she smirked.

Dean Hyphen-Lugosi said the University was sensitive to male students' complaints that the policy is discriminatory. "That's why we dropped the requirement that they wear the collars around their [genitals]," she explained. "That was a major concession by our female students, and especially by the faculty in our Women's Studies department, because they were very much looking forward to seeing the boys' reactions when they crossed *that* line."

MERCHANT SNAGS PULITZER WITH "BACK IN 5 MINUTES" SIGN

PHILADELPHIA - Ron Vassel of Ron's Computer Repair in Rittenhouse Square was awarded the Pulitzer Prize in General Non-Fiction for the sign he puts on his shop door to alert customers that he'll be "Back in Five Minutes -- Gone to the Restroom."

A Pulitzer Committee Member called the note "a groundbreaking masterwork -- a succinct yet sweeping narrative of isolation and alienation, fraught with the tension that can evolve only from the intersection of emotional and physiological frisson, everywhere signifying the urological erasure of one's own frail and bitter humanity."

In his acceptance speech, Vassel thanked his loyal customers, the Pulitzer committee, the Coca-Cola company, and the makers of Flomax.

MONET'S ONE REGRET: "GARDEN AT SAINTE ADRESSE"

PARIS - Long lost letters from Claude Monet to his tailor, Jacques Mendelbaum, revealed that the French Impressionist considered his landmark work Garden at Sainte Adresse to be "a disaster."

"I stood by my canvas for 16 hours straight," wrote Monet, "waiting in vain for the bastards cluttering up the scene to leave. They did not, so I was forced to paint the damn thing with them in it."

Monet revealed that he gave "serious consideration" to murdering "the broads with the umbrellas" who refused to move. He also "came perilously close" to "dumping" the seated, hat-wearing man "into the briny deep where, to my delight, his testicles would have been devoured by sharks."

When a sailboat dropped anchor directly in front of him, Monet could stand no more. so he climbed atop the railing overlooking the sea and challenged the captain to a fight to the death. "Do you know who I am? I'm Claude F***ing Monet, foremost artist in the world! You -- and these f***ing bastards decked out in the expensive clothes -- are ruining my art!"

Art historians say that the letters provide important context that explains the handwritten note Monet scrawled on the backside of the canvas: "Do not display -- trash!"

*CARBOLIC*BREAKING*NEWS:*

AL GORE TO MEDIATE PEACE TALKS BETWEEN HEAT MISER, SNOW MISER

CEO OF MATTEL SUPPLIER RESPONSIBLE FOR TOY RECALL COMMITS SUICIDE BY FORCING HEAD INTO EASY BAKE OVEN

VIRGIN MARY CLAIMS CHEETO LOOKS EXACTLY LIKE MASSAGE THERAPIST FROM KANSAS CITY

Blessed Mother says she plans to sell it on eBay

CHINESE TOY MAKER APOLOGIZES FOR DATE RAPE SCANDAL

Barbie Doll found to contain date-rape drug; Ken and G.I. Joe had their way with her

AFTER 66 YEARS, AMERICA'S GREATEST FILM FINALLY GETS A SEQUEL

Citizen Kane 2: Rosebud's Revenge opens in select cities next year;
producer James Wan promises "a lot more blood and gore this time"

MAYO CLINIC: PATIENTS WILL NOW "PAY THROUGH THE NOSE" FOR BRAIN SURGERY THROUGH THE NOSE

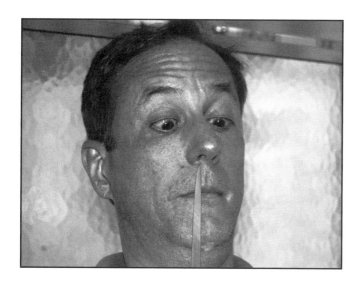

MTV CONCEDES "REAL WORLD BAGHDAD" "NOT SUCH A GOOD IDEA" AFTER BOMB DECIMATES ROOMMATES' COOL LOFT, KILLING FOUR ANGST-RIDDEN CAST MEMBERS

Network executives admit bombing gives tired series "much-needed cachet"

TV HIGHLIGHTS: "THE MAN WHO SHOT LINCOLN," STARRING BURT WARD

Actor's insistence on playing John Wilkes Booth in "Robin" costume mars film

HOLLYWOOD - "The Man Who Shot Lincoln" airing tonight, the anniversary of assassination of America's 16th President, is a gritty and shockingly realistic portrayal of the events leading up the April 14, 1865 assassination of President Abraham Lincoln by John Wilkes Booth, a well-known and flamboyant actor of his day.

The documentary marks the return to prime time television of Burt Ward, who plays Booth. Ward is best known for portraying "Robin, the Boy Wonder," opposite Adam West in the 1960's camp TV classic, "Batman."

Ward insisted on playing Booth in his old "Robin" costume, and the results are mixed. At first, the colorful costume proves somewhat of a distraction, but Ward's performance is so self-assured and his screen presence so commanding that ultimately it doesn't matter.

Ward's old mannerisms are still there, and they still work like a charm, from the quick-tempered habit of punching his fist into his other hand to blurting out "Holy states' rights!" in one key scene.

Women and gay viewers will find his leap from the balcony at Fords Theater following the shooting utterly mesmerizing. (Let's just say the tights have never been tighter.) There is good reason he was once called the "Boy Wonder."

All in all, this is the most realistic documentary of the Lincoln assassination ever made. Be forewarned: the violence of the actual shooting is palpable, vividly enhanced by the giant cartoon "POW" that bursts across the screen when Ward fires the gun.

Actor Charles Durning is a noble Lincoln, and Bette Midler provides welcome comic relief as nutty Mary Todd Lincoln. My only qualm is that the three-hour running time is altogether too short. This film, airing on CBS at 8 p.m. Eastern Time, is not to be missed.

CARBOLICBREAKINGNEWS:

COMIC STRIP STAR CALVIN, IMPRISONED FOR PUBLIC URINATION, MURDERED BY FELLOW INMATE

OPRAH'S BOOK CLUB ANNOUNCES NEXT SELECTION

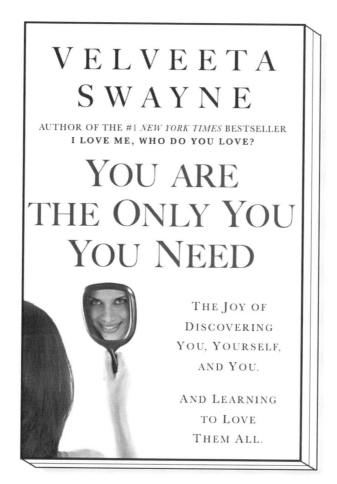

STUDY REVEALS ALL WOMEN WILL BE SEXUALLY ASSAULTED IN THEIR LIFETIMES

Researchers dismiss widely accepted 1-in-4 figure: "The authors of those studies obviously hated women"

BRAD PITT AND ANGELINA JOLIE HAVE TWINS, GIVE THEM UP FOR ADOPTION

CARBOLIC SCIENCE CORNER:
The Most Germ-Infested Object in Your Home is Your Soap!

By Dr. Noah Swayne, Scientist

There's an enemy hiding in your bathroom's soap dish. It wants you to hold it, to caress it, to think that only it can make you clean. In fact, it is the single most germ-infested object in your home.

It is your soap.

I am, of course, speaking from a purely SCIENTIFIC perspective.

Each and every day, you invite this bacteria-encrusted Trojan Horse into the most private room of your home, the room where you frolic about naked in front of the mirror longing for a longer long john, blissfully oblivious that the thing that's supposed to protect you from filth and disease is actually laden through and through with them.

One of the best-kept modern medical secrets is that soap -- yes, soap -- has been the leading cause of death in America for the past sixty-seven years.

Men, do you hate to get urine on your hands when you pee? You should know that urine contains .0001 mg of germs per square inch. Soap contains 8.73 mg of germs per square inch. You'd be much more sanitary if you washed your hands with pee instead of soap.

Vomit, industrial waste, and rodents are all more sanitary than soap.

There is only one solution if you want to avoid disease and, yes, even death: ditch the soap. Fast. The next time someone pesters you to wash your hands, just point out these simple, SCIENTIFIC facts.

CARBOLICHEALTHNEWS:

FDA ACCUSES CIALIS OF FALSE ADVERTISING

"In all of our clinical trials," FDA Commissioner Andrew von Eschenbach said, "the drug never once enabled a man and woman to get it on while sitting in separate bathtubs"

"BULL DAY" AT THE CHIHULY GLASS EXHIBITION TURNS TRAGIC

PITTSBURGH -- Artist Dale Chihuly must be thinking his exhibition of glass sculptures at Phipps Conservatory is snake-bitten. First were the many fires ignited by concentrated beams of sunlight refracted through Chihuly's masterpieces, a story reported only by this news source. That problem worked itself out when Pittsburgh's usual cloudy weather returned after a freakish period of sunshine.

The latest fiasco started innocently enough. Phipps Director of Glass, Atilla Khan, wanted to attract glass aficionados from some of the outlying rural counties, so he declared last Saturday "Bring Your Bull to Phipps Day" and offered free admission to any youngster accompanied by an adult male bovine. Bull moose and elk were also acceptable.

"Allegheny County doesn't have anything like a county fair anymore," Khan explained, "I figure what the hell -- this [event] could be fun."

The event was far from fun. Just ask 10-year old Billy Ambrose from Masontown, Fayette County. No sooner had he entered Phipps with his prize bull, Peter Ustinov, than the trouble started. It turned out that "PU," as Billy calls him, is allergic to some of the plants at Phipps and began to sneeze.

"There's not much room for a bull to sneeze in there," said Billy's mother, Anna, "so PU just ran amok."

PU flattened one sculpture after another, sending glass flying everywhere. "It was like a bull in a china shop," one witness observed. Hundreds of people were cut. "There was blood -- blood everywhere," Billy related between sobs.

It took doctors at Mercy Hospital several hours to patch up the injured. Thirty-eight people remain hospitalized.

Khan said Phipps will have counselors available for the injured and plans to make it up to them with a special "Lacerations Day" over the Labor Day Weekend.

CARBOLICBREAKINGNEWS:

ACLU OBTAINS INJUNCTION TO STOP LINUS FROM RECITING SCRIPTURE ON SCHOOL PROPERTY

MR. BLACKWELL NAMES ABU GHRAIB PRISONER WORST-DRESSED OF THE YEAR; BRITNEY SPEARS A CLOSE SECOND

SAUDI ARABIAN OFFICIALS PROTEST CONTROVERSIAL "MARY WORTH" STRIP IN WHICH MARY HAS COFFEE WITH THE PROPHET MOHAMMED

LOCAL ENTREPRENEUR STILL PECKING AWAY

PENNSYLVANIA GOVERNOR ED RENDELL NARROWLY DEFEATS FORMER VICE PRESIDENT AL GORE IN OVERTIME AT THIS YEAR'S CONEY ISLAND HOT-DOG EATING CONTEST

BARBARA WALTERS NAMES LOCAL PLUMBER BRUCE MURRAY ONE OF "TEN MOST FASCINATING PEOPLE OF THE YEAR"

NEW YORK - Barbara Walters will profile her picks for the ten most fascinating people of the year tonight on ABC at 10 p.m. EST, and there's a surprise in the line-up.

Bruce Murray, a Johnstown, Pennsylvania, plumber who only twice in his life strayed more than forty miles from home, will join Tom Cruise, Condeleeza Rice, child star Dakota Fanning, and six others on the show.

Murray said he has no idea why Ms. Walters wants to profile him, but noted that he did take piano lessons as a child and retains aspirations of being a sports agent. "Maybe they're putting me on the TV [show] as a sort of, you know, beacon or what have you, to, you know, show people that you can still have dreams in this country, or whatever," Murray said.

We caught up with Ms. Walters and asked her why a Johnstown plumber had been named one of the year's most fascinating people. A look of horror mixed with disgust leapt across her face, as if this were the first she'd heard of it. She quickly recovered and explained that Murray "represents the working American, the backbone of our country."

Although Murray said he wants to meet Dakota Fanning, ABC ruled that out because it turns out Murray is a convicted sex offender, having once molested two children while on a toilet repair job.

REVEALED: ACTRESS DEBORAH KERR'S LIP-SYNCHED DYING WORDS DUBBED BY MARNI NIXON

LONDON - Deborah Kerr, who danced with the Siamese monarch played by Yul Brynner in *The King and I*, has died. She was 86.

Ms. Kerr did not do her own singing in the classic musical; she lip-synched the songs, which were dubbed by veteran singer Marni Nixon, who was also the singing voice for Audrey Hepburn in the film version of *My Fair Lady* and for Natalie Wood in *West Side Story*.

As Ms. Kerr lay dying, she called for Ms. Nixon, who arrived at her bedside moments before the end. Ms Kerr handed Ms. Nixon a prepared text labeled "dying words." Ms. Nixon tearfully read the document as Ms. Kerr lip-synched it, then expired.

ABBOTT AND COSTELLO'S "WHO'S ON FIRST" ROUTINE, RECITED BACKWARD, IS SATANIC CHANT TO RAISE THE DEAD

When Abbott says, "I Don't Know's on third," that's the cue for the human sacrifice

HOLLYWOOD - The buffoonish comedy team of Abbott and Costello reigned supreme as the most popular act in show business in the 1940s and early 1950s, proving beloved by children and grandparents alike. But a new book reveals that the seemingly innocent clowns were, in fact, serious disciples of the most sinister forces of the occult.

Dr. Bradleys Roadhouse, Professor of Anthropology at Crystal State University, says in his landmark book, *Who's on First? Lucifer!*, that when Abbott and Costello's most popular routine, "Who's on First," is played backward, it reveals a chant, dating to the third century A.D., commonly recited by worshippers of Satan in an unholy ritual to raise the dead.

"The part in the routine where Abbott says, 'I Don't Know's on third,' when played backward, is the cue for the Seven Corpses of Osiris to perform a ghastly human sacrifice. Believe me, there is nothing funny about that," Professor Roadhouse said.

In his next book, Dr. Roadhouse will chronicle head "Three Stooge" Moe Howard's lifelong attempts to master the art of voodoo in the hopes of inflicting greater pain on his fellow Stooges.

CARBOLICBREAKINGNEWS:

NEXT YEAR'S SUPER BOWL PRE-GAME SHOW SLATED TO BEGIN ON AUGUST 16TH

BRAD PITT AND ANGELINA JOLIE TO ADOPT EIGHT MORE CHILDREN, INCLUDING "TODAY SHOW" ANCHOR ANN CURRY

"She's always following us around and begging for interviews," Jolie said, "so we figured we "may as well just give her a room of her own."

DEPARTMENT OF HOMELAND SECURITY ISSUES NEW TERROR ALERT ADVISORY FOR SUBURBS, MIDDLE AMERICA

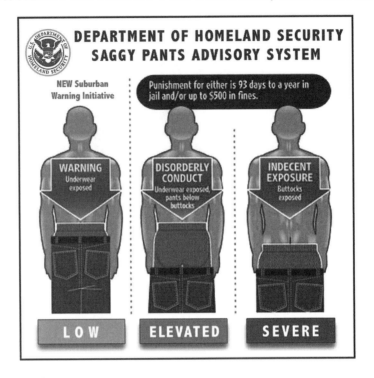

GAY COWBOY FILM "BROKEBACK MOUNTAIN" WINS 3 OSCARS; SMALL EARTHQUAKE FELT BENEATH NEWPORT BEACH GRAVESTONE

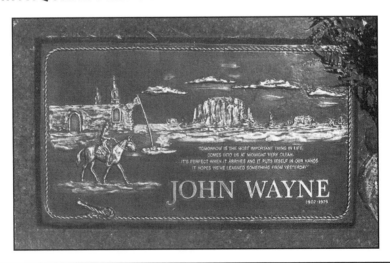

FAMED NEW ORLEANS PAINTER CREATES 2008 MARDI GRAS COMMEMORATIVE ARTWORK: *PEEING ON BOURBON STREET*

Noah Swayne's delightful depiction of three boys publicly urinating will be sold for just $199; the painting, a companion piece to last year's acclaimed *Peeing on Canal Street*, is the third installment of the artist's *Peeing All Over the Big Easy* masterwork

CARBOLICBREAKINGNEWS:

JOE BARBERA, "FLINTSTONES" PRODUCER, DEAD AT 95

On half-mile ride to cemetery, hearse passes same crudely drawn house and cactus forty-seven times

FOUND: LOUIS FARRAKHAN'S LOST RECORDING OF "WHITE CHRISTMAS"

NEW FOX SERIES: PEOPLE SAY THE DAMNEDEST THINGS IN CONFESSION!

NEW YORK - The Vatican today called on people of goodwill to boycott the Fox Network's new reality show, "People Say the Damnedest Things in Confession!," which puts hidden cameras and microphones in the confessional of a Catholic Church.

"It captures on tape the most intimate sins of the penitents for the viewing pleasure of Fox's hedonistic young audience," said the show's producer Larry Bang. "But it's all done in good taste."

In one segment of the premiere, a young man confesses to having sex with his girlfriend out of wedlock. Later that day, the show's producers show the confession to the girlfriend, "and that's where the fireworks begin," Bang chuckles.

"She confronts the guy, and she is just livid. 'So you think what we do is wrong,' she yells. Well, the sheepish look on his face is just priceless. But then later that night, he gets back at her. They're sitting on her couch, and she's still upset with him, pouting and all that. Then the doorbell rings, and in comes an exorcist -- one of our actors dressed like a priest -- and he proceeds to do an exorcism on this young woman to cast out her demons, you know, for tempting this guy and all. Well, that sends her over the edge. She throws them both out, and the boyfriend can't stop laughing."

"So you see," Bang chortles, "the whole thing's very healthy."

CARBOLICBREAKINGNEWS:

CRITICS PAN LATEST EPISODE OF "24," COMPLAIN THAT JACK BAUER WAITING IN EMERGENCY ROOM FOR ONE HOUR "LACKS DRAMATIC TENSION"

SACHEEN LITTLEFEATHER ARRIVES AT PIZZA HUT, READS PREPARED STATEMENT EXPLAINING WHY MARLON BRANDO WON'T APPEAR TO PICK UP HIS ORDER

"Mr. Brando will not be appearing to pick up his pizza in protest of the ongoing siege at Wounded Knee, not mention the fast food industry's misrepresentation of American Indians in its advertising. Instead, Mr. Brando has asked me to deliver the pizza to his house, with plenty of extra napkins and two liters of Coke."

*CARBOLIC*BREAKING*NEWS:*

JEAN CLAUDE VAN DAMME TO HOST *A KICK-BOXING CHRISTMAS*, FEATURING "PLENTY OF KICKING, CAROLING"

FBI: SON WHO SAW MOMMY KISSING SANTA CLAUS HAS BEEN SHAKING THE OLD WOMAN DOWN SINCE 1952

POSTMASTER LICKS NEW SINATRA STAMP; STAMP KNOCKS OUT THREE OF HIS TEETH

HYPOCRITES SOCIETY QUESTIONS NEW MEMBERS' SINCERITY

CARBOLICSMOKEBALL

presents

ZOMBIES ATE MY OPINIONS

EXCESSIVE SHAKING AT BALLPARK URINAL IS APPALLING
Guest Commentary by Supreme Court Justice Harry Blackmun

I rarely have occasion to utilize a crowded public restroom, but in the seventh inning stretch of last Sunday's game between the Pirates and the Astros at Pittsburgh's PNC Park, I strolled down from the Carbolic Smoke Ball box behind home plate to visit with vendor T.C. Congdon, who was working near the visitor's dugout. (Whenever I am in town, I confer with Mr. Congdon on cases pending before the United States Supreme Court.) Before venturing back upstairs, I decided to stop at the restroom, an experience that is forever etched into my memory.

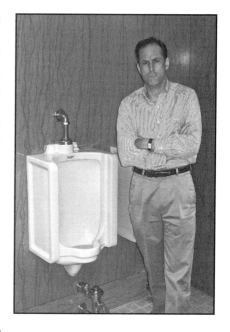

While I was standing at the urinal, two college-aged men assumed spots at the urinals immediately to my right. They were conversing in the inane style of that age group, peppering every sentence of their idiotic dialogue with the word "like." They prattled on about mammary glands and the female canal leading from the uterus, undoubtedly the only biological concepts of which they have any understanding. When they had finished emptying what once was illegally imbibed beer from their underaged bladders, one of the young men immediately fled out the door in the *de rigueur* fashion of that age group without washing his hands. My mind instinctively conjured up all manner of hideous scenario involving those bacteria-laden claws groping some unsuspecting young woman.

As repellent as that spectacle was, it was nothing compared to what was about to occur. The other young man, the one immediately next to me, proceeded to perform an act that can only be described as appalling.

Please understand that at all pertinent times, in accordance with proper urinal etiquette, my eyes were pointed straight ahead. But damn my peripheral vision! Despite my best efforts, I could not help but notice that when the young man had finished his task, he began to shake his instrument as is customary in such circumstances. I shall spare our female readers excessive description of this strange male ritual, but suffice it to say that the maximum allowable shakes is four. There is ample Supreme Court precedent to that effect.

But this particular young man did not stop at four. He did four, then seven, then -- I stopped counting. Worse, he was not content with merely shaking it. It became a sort of whip as he spastically snapped it forward with such rapidity that I seriously thought it would generate a sonic boom, the first body part to break the sound barrier. Somewhere in the course of this horror show, he began to twirl the offending appendage in a manner usually reserved for the tassels of busty female strippers. **(cont. on p. 154)**

BLACKMUN: EXCESSIVE SHAKING AT BALLPARK URINAL IS APPALLING

(cont. from p. 153) I wish I could say the spray did not splatter my glasses, but that would be untrue.

There was, of course, no legitimate reason for this revolting display of penile calisthenics. I could not help but think that this urinal, constructed to serve a useful purpose, had been transmogrified into a near-occasion of sin.

Thankfully, I was able to depart the room without further witness to this nauseating exhibition. For all I know, the boy is still in there shaking away.

You see, it isn't enough that the members of this generation of nitwits have desecrated the English language, abandoned religion because it does not add to their immediate gratification (and because religion disapproves of conduct that *does* add to their immediate gratification), and transformed their wholesale lack of taste in music, literature, art, and motion pictures into the very engines that drive capitalism. No, this young man's misconduct was an example of the singular failing that invariably signals the decline and eventual collapse of a great society: ignorance of proper urinal etiquette.

I am sorry to say we are doomed. And the Pirates lost to the Astros, 1-0.

The Hon. Harry Blackmun
Associate Justice, United States Supreme Court

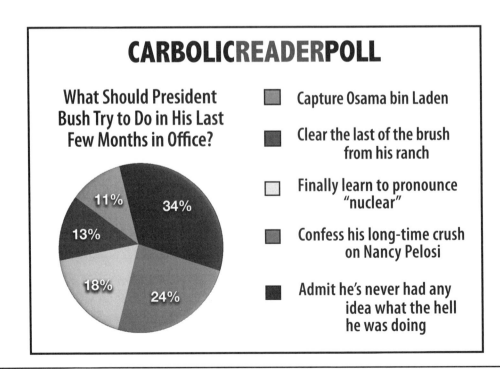

CARBOLIC FLASHBACK: SEPTEMBER 10TH, 2001: "IT'S ABOUT TIME THE UNITED STATES STOPPED WORRYING ABOUT INCONSEQUENTIAL OSAMA BIN LADEN"

Commentary by Carbolic Smoke Ball Editor, The Honorable Rufus Peckham

NEW YORK - It is rarely spoken about, even in the furtive corridors of the CIA building. Our elected officials invariably deny it. But this office has obtained proof positive, in the form of a secret memo from CIA Director George Tenet, that the United States "has declared war."

With whom exactly are we at war? Russia? China? North Korea? None of the above. We are "at war" not with a nation but with a person, indeed someone few Americans have ever even heard of. Someone who is not a threat to us. As preposterous as it sounds, the most powerful nation in the history of the world is "at war" with an innocuous nomadic Muslim fanatic named Osama bin Laden.

Bin Laden has no army, only meager resources, and from what I can tell after studying the situation closely, only good intentions toward the United States. It is obvious to any rational person that we should not be "at war" with this person.

But the CIA is concocting all manner of doomsday scenario to panic us; the most absurd being that bin Laden intends to use our own airplanes as weapons against us. This cannot and will not happen.

When was the last time you heard of an American jetliner being hijacked to Havana? It used to happen practically daily, but with high-tech metal detectors in place, our airports have become invulnerable to sabotage. (There is a feeling among some that the CIA wants to scare us so that they can insist upon unnecessary security measures at our airports. One of the most laughable would require us to remove our shoes as we proceed through the metal detectors. This might be acceptable in Japan where removing shoes is a national fetish, but it will never happen here.)

The fact is we could track down and destroy bin Laden and his puny band of supporters any time we wanted to. And if he dared try anything at all, the whole world -- France, Germany, you name it -- would back us 150% in obliterating the Muslin nations of our choice. Bin Laden would not dare do that to his own people. In any event, the Muslim people would not allow bin Laden to bring harm to us. They love the United States too much; they love Western culture too much.

It is time we put the CIA's resources to better use than to harass this little flea, this nothing, Osama bin what's-his-name.

CARBOLIC FLASHBACK: JULY 3, 1776: "REJOICE, DEAR READERS, FOR WE SHALL ALWAYS BE ENGLISHMEN!"

Commentary by Carbolic Smoke Ball Editor, The Honorable Josiah Peckham

Last month, Richard Henry Lee, a delegate to the Second Continental Congress from Virginia, proposed a resolution that, if passed, would dissolve the colonies' ties with their motherland.

Readers of this publication know my feelings about this resolution and its sponsor, so I will not repeat them here. The resolution is a cesspool, an open sewer, a pit of putrefaction, a treasonous, slimy gathering of all that is rotten in the debris of human depravity. And in the center of all this waste and stench, besmearing himself with its foulest defilement, splashes, leaps, cavorts and wallows a bifurcated specimen, lurks a villainous traitor who responds to the name of Richard Henry Lee.

Fortunately, I have just come from Philadelphia, where I've conferred with the members of the Second Continental Congress and have learned beyond all doubt that this Lee Resolution is as dead as a doornail. You heard it here first.

My dear friend John Adams assured me that although a committee has been formed supposedly to draft a declaration of independence, it is a sham, concocted to satisfy the advocates of independence without any intention of acting. To ensure the failure of such a declaration, a small cabal of influential men on the committee has delegated the writing of the document to an insubstantial, coquettish young delegate from Virginia by the name of Thomas Jefferson. Mr. Adams assures me the young man will never amount to anything, and that his command of the language is slight at best.

Mr. Adams said I should publish this useful information for the benefit and edification of my many readers. I thanked Mr. Adams for this, and for putting behind us that little incident from last November between me and Abigail when I found myself in Boston (not to repeat ourself, but it was cold, and I had nowhere else to sleep). I am glad Mr. Adams is not vindictive.

No, dear readers, one-hundred, nay, two-hundred years from now and beyond, the misguided devotees of independence will have been long forgotten, and we shall rejoice, as we now rejoice, and as we always have rejoiced, that we are Englishmen!

CARBOLIC FLASHBACK: MARCH 17, 1845: "IF THERE'S ONE THING WE IRISH CAN COUNT ON, IT'S THE POTATO"

Commentary by Carbolic Smoke Ball Editor Horace Peckham

Well now, I'll begin at the beginnin', says I, and here, on the feast to honor himself, Saint Patrick, no less. Instead of telling it to you in the Irish, as is my custom, I'll spell it out in English so that even the sons of Cromwell can read what I've got to say.

In a world where change is practically the only constant, every century a new technological advance, so-called, turns us upside down, from the wondrous improvements in smelting, to this dizzying cotton spinning, to the steam engine itself. Why, aside from change, the only other thing we Irish can depend on with absolute certainty is, of course, our national staple, the potato. Starch, starch and more starch. There's nothing better for you if you're Irish, you know. We could not live without it, but we needn't ever worry about that.

Now the reason I'm writing. Some of the peevish sons of Cromwell are up to their old shenanigans trying to scare the good people of Ireland into leaving. It's not enough for them that they took our land, lo the many years ago. Their latest deceit, so I am told, is to convince our people that a fungi is spreading across the nation's potato crop, a blight on the land that, they say, will quickly destroy each and every potato throughout all of Ireland. This, they assert, will lead to the death, or worse, the emigration, of millions of our people. Some of these Protestant liars are making the assertion that hundreds of thousands of our people will end up in a backwater land such as America.

Now how ridiculous is this? It is, in fact, a stark lie, bald-faced and all, and you heard it here first. The ones who are uttering these things will regret it till their dying day, if they should live that long. The potato is the *raison d'etre*, the *sine qua non* of Ireland. Like the land and the sea, the potato will always be, unchanged, immutable. I say it again, as I say it in this column each and every day, the only blight on our land remains the cesspool that was Oliver Cromwell, almost two hundred years after his malefactions against God and our people.

As goes the ancient saying that seems to fit every occasion, and really none at all: "The lad set sail a mere youth, on a youth's voyage, but when he returned, he was -- an Irishman!" And so must it be here.

And now I'll be sayin' good day to you.

CARBOLIC FLASHBACK: DECEMBER 6, 1941: THE ONLY THING WE HAVE TO FEAR FROM THE JAPANESE IS FEAR OF THE JAPANESE ITSELF

Commentary by Carbolic Smoke Ball Editor, The Honorable Rufus Peckham

The State Department is up to its old shenanigans, concocting all manner of artifice to goad, cajole, wheedle and incite the gentle and peace-loving people of Japan into attacking the United States of America. Less than two weeks ago, our Secretary of State Cordell Hull unilaterally demanded that the Japanese withdraw all their troops from China in an attempt to provoke a Japanese attack.

It won't happen. The Japanese will, of course, never attack the United States of America, despite whatever geopolitical legerdemain the State Department employs. You heard it here first.

I have studied the Japanese closely for many years, their quaint ways and inscrutable customs, and I am certain beyond any reasonable doubt that Japan would immediately drop any designs it has on mainland China if it meant militarily tangling with us. The fact of the matter is, the Japanese care not a whit about whether they lose face in the international community by backing down when pushed. Trust me on this one.

I am also thoroughly familiar with the Japanese military, and I am certain that they do not possess the capability of launching an attack on our Pacific fleet, and they know it. Moreover, I have personally met their Imperial General Hideki Tojo (he once gave me a recipe for raisin bread), and I found him to be a fun-loving, gregarious man more concerned with peace than any so-called imperial designs.

No further exegesis on this point is warranted, since the thing the State Department seems bent on inciting simply is an impossibility.

Now, whether the Japanese should withdraw from China is another matter. No useful purpose would be served by responding to the self-serving blather of Secretary of State Cordell Hull's November 26 note to the Japanese that demanded their complete withdrawal from mainland China. Japan has expended tremendous national resources to dominate China, and Hull would completely eviscerate all of that hard work. The domination Japan seeks is part and parcel of its larger expansionist interests, which may not be such a bad thing, truth be told.

But that is the subject of another editorial. For now, it is my opinion that the American people are bored to tears with this Japanese topic, and I will not bother them further with it.

CARBOLIC FLASHBACK: JUNE 4, 1968: LIVE FROM THE AMBASSADOR HOTEL

Commentary by Carbolic Smoke Ball Editor, The Honorable Rufus Peckham

I am bursting with excitement as I write this! I am in Los Angeles today, because I am coordinating tonight's victory celebration for Sen. Robert F. Kennedy at the Ambassador Hotel. I predict the Senator will score a decisive victory in today's California primary and that we'll have reasons-a-plenty to celebrate tonight.

The Senator's aides wanted the party to be held at the Beverly Hills Hilton, because they claimed the "security" is better there, but I prevailed, and the party will be here at the Ambassador. (I thought the Senator might enjoy being here, because this is the same hotel where Nixon wrote his Checkers speech in 1952.)

Anyway, there is no necessity for "security" of any kind. Up and down the state, the Senator is beloved by everyone. Did President Kennedy have need of security in Dallas, except for one lone nut? The President was beloved by everyone except for Mr. Lee "I Hate President Kennedy" Oswald. I am happy to report that Mr. Oswald is resting six feet under the earth, thanks to Mr. Jack Ruby, so he will be no threat here tonight. I gave the Kennedy people my word: if the Senator needs any security at all, I'll provide it myself. And you heard it here first.

In any event, I've made all the arrangements for tonight. He'll address his adoring supporters and tell them, "It's on to Chicago!" I will then usher him through the kitchen, because I want him to meet the oppressed and subjugated kitchen workers. I checked out the area yesterday, and it will be a perfect spot for the Senator to engage in a Q & A with some real working folks, people with beefs about all sorts of things, angry people.

One young Palestinian man I spoke with said he's looking forward to being there so he can personally let the Senator know how he feels about the Senator's views on Israeli-Palestinian relations. That's exactly what we need! Some real sparks! He asked me where he should stand, so I showed him the perfect spot where he can get close to the Senator.

I'll then usher the Senator into a media room where — and I don't think I'm speaking out of school here — he'll announce that he's asked me to run on his ticket as Vice President.

So, in a few minutes, it's on to Chicago! And then . . . to the White House!

Nothing can stop us now!

STAGE REVIEW: "THE URINAL MONOLOGUES" MIGHT PISS YOU OFF

Noe Givven-Tayke, Carbolic Theater Critic

The Urinal Monologues, a series of interlocking monologues by six talking urinals dealing with all-things-penis, is perhaps the first serious attempt to unlock the urinal's inner voice.

The show, making its world debut in the men's room of the City Theater, is a cathartic, gut-wrenching celebration of the unspoken truths about the penis: that it is the only tool through which men achieve both solidarity with maleness and, paradoxically, total individuality, yet society ordains it remain zippered out of sight due to its sublime power for both procreation and violence. Aside from that, we are told that it's a lot of fun to use it to take a whizz in the snow.

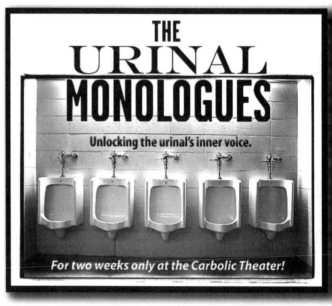

These themes are explored with unflinching candor in monologues dealing with the gender-specific oppression men experience when they are forced to shake after peeing to avoid getting urine drip on their underwear, not to mention the unspeakable shame of morning erections.

But a few women in the audience found it a little off-putting when one urinal encouraged the audience to repeatedly chant the phrase "piss on women." One young female in the audience later said that the chant did little to empower men and only served to dilute the play's important message of urging men to embrace their genitalia with both hands. Some of the men who participated in the chant admitted they were embarrassed by their actions but said they'd probably do it again if given the chance. In fact, the chant was intended by playwright Geraldine Jones to instill a sense of collective male guilt, but the men who spoke with us said that concept was completely foreign to them.

The ending more than made up for any failings, though, as the men in the audience threw down their inhibitions and approached the urinals, slowly at first, then with greater confidence. One by one they unzipped, some with beer in hand, and like race horses, peed to rousing applause. More than a few raised both arms while they pissed in a triumphant gesture of masculinity, a fitting coda to a play that epitomizes everything that modern theater does right. The triumph was topped off by an inspired blast of realism when, after the men had finished urinating, women in the audience had to remind most of them to wash their hands.

CARBOLIC MOVE REVIEW: *TEETH*, A FOUR-LIPPED MAN-EATER THAT DISMEMBERS NAUGHTY MEMBERS

Lorena Bobbitt, Carbolic Film Critic

Mitchell Lichtenstein's *Teeth* is a rapturous feminist call to bloodlust, a vengeance porno flick with the soul of a grindhouse potboiler, and the greatest male-bashing -- or more accurately, male-chomping -- feast ever served up by Hollywood. For those living under a rock or born with a Y chromosome (pretty much the same thing), this is a modern-day retelling of the *vagina dentata* fable about a high school girl

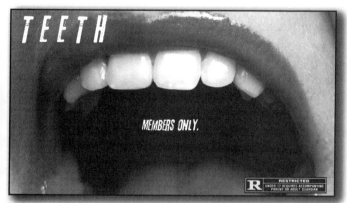

who discovers that her whooha has grown choppers that bite off the tallywacker of any young man foolish enough to abuse her. Our heroine, brilliantly played by perky-breasted Jess Weixler (who does get naked), is initially terrified of her body but soon realizes her fish factory is a tool for feminine empowerment, the leveler of patriarchy.

The young men in the audience at Friday's opening howled with shocked laughter each time the doo-dads of one of their cinematic counterparts ended up on the floor. I suppose they've never seen a severed penis up close before. The biggest roar came when John Hensley's vicious dog happily munched on his master's meat missile whilst the emasculated poor thing could do nothing but watch. The camera, thankfully, leaves nothing to the imagination.

I watched the film from a purely technical perspective. I must say, each of the severed penises were carved with admirable precision. I won't bore the readers with inside baseball stuff about slicing penises -- about how a dull instrument can ruin the most beautiful meat, or the importance of cutting against the grain, or the fact that you must firmly anchor your guy's beef stick before cutting -- suffice it to say that Ms. Weixler's vagina-teeth produced the most beautiful presentation of severed penises I have ever seen, and I am an authority.

The astute producers of *Teeth* know a good thing when they see it, so they've greenlit a sequel called "Braces." It's the story of a noble feminist orthodontist who fits Ms. Weixler's choppers with a set of sweet-looking braces to adjust a nasty malocclusion that makes penis-chomping uncomfortable.

The only drawback to *Teeth* is Mr. Lichtenstein's disclaimer, "no men were harmed during the making of this film." Oh, well, we can't have everything.

Nevertheless, I give this one Four Breasts.

CARBOLIC MOVIE REVIEW: THE LONG-AWAITED *CITIZEN KANE* SEQUEL, *CK2: ROSEBUD'S REVENGE*

Barry Paris, Carbolic Film Critic

When last we saw Rosebud, the most famous sled in all of filmdom, she was burning in the citizen flames of the stately Xanadu boiler room. Now, forty-six years later, she's risen phoenix-like from the ashes of movie history and Charles Foster's mansion to carry on her centuries-long reign of terror. A prologue, stylishly shot in black-and-white and Tolandesque deep focus, reveals that Rosebud was first constructed during the French Revolution, as a gift from the King and Queen to their darling, devilish little Dauphin. But faster than you can say "Ski the Bastille!," the King and Queen are eating cake and losing their heads, run through with those nasty, rusty runners while blood splatters the screen and shrieking French curse words fill the air.

After the opening credits (think Saul Bass meets David Fincher), we're back in Kane's basement warehouse, watching one of those silhouetted reporters pull that menacing sled from the fire and promise to donate it to an orphanage in Miami. But we're not in Xanadu anymore, Frodo; there won't be any sunshine or blue skies where that sled appears. The 95-minute forecast is for dark and stormy nights, with a 100-percent chance of blood, gore, and graphic dismemberments.

Sarah Michelle Gellar stars as Buffy Bernstein, a former bobsled-rider and current star reporter who investigates a series of brutal murders in New York City and soon realizes that these sleigh-ings may have something to do with her own haunted past. Gellar takes her role seriously enough to make us do the same from time to time. She has a mildly interesting subplot with a charming lawyer (Freddie Prinze Jr.) who sweet-talks her into bed, then sour-talks her into chasing after the sled. Could he have a secret longing in his past too?

The script's prose is arguably a degree or two snappier than that in the Yellow Pages. Which is apropos, since the *New York Inquirer* in the original film was a searing commentary on the Yellow Journalism of William Randolph Hearst and his *New York Journal*, which was surely not as interesting as the journal I kept while writing biographies of Greta Garbo, Louise Brooks, and Audrey Hepburn, all of which — the biographies, not the actresses — are available at Amazon.com.

I digress. But I shall try not to regress. Unless I am stressed. Or under duress. O-Kane?! **(cont. on p. 163)**

CARBOLIC MOVE REVIEW: CK2: ROSEBUD'S REVENGE

(cont. from p. 162) Director Hideo Nakata, the head of this "Kane" mutiny, gives precious little help with his predictably fragmented photography and choppy editing. This film may as well have been cut at a sushi bar. Yes, it's that fishy. And smelly.

Now don't get me wrong. If you knew sushi like I know sushi, especially at Pacific Ring in Squirrel Hill, you'd like it. But you still wouldn't like this film. Or its over-the-top finale, in which the now romantically entangled grandchildren of Mr. Leland and Mr. Bernstein try to outlive their curse and destroy that thorny sled forever by setting it on fire, throwing it over a cliff, and battling its army of sled-dog zombies in the Iditarod from Hell.

Where is Orson Welles when we need him? Well, in all fairness, he's dead. Just like all of the people I write about. But there must be some living writer-directors who could and should come to the rescue of great films desperately seeking horror movie sequels worthy of them.

Still, it doesn't do much good to kvetch about kvality. This generation of the Brothers Warner — would that be the Warner Great-Grandsons? -- is betting there are enough gore hounds and Kane-y cats out there to return its "Rosebud's Revenge" investment. I'm betting they're right, and that it won't be long before we see *Citizen Kane 3: Sled II*. Because these days, nothing sells like bloody horror and edgy, unnecessary sequels from aptly named producers like James Wan.

Oh, well. What Xan a critic du?

CSB'S LIST OF THE TOP 10 ALL-TIME GREATEST FIRST DRAFTS OF FAMOUS, BUT NOT QUITE AS GOOD AS THE ORIGINALS, MOVIE LINES

10. "Go ahead, make my bed." (*Sudden Impact*)

9. "I'll make him an offer that'll get the negotiations going." (*The Godfather*)

8. "Luke, I am your former next-door neighbor, Irving Mendelbaum." (*The Empire Strikes Back*)

7. "I'm mad as hell, and I just might do something about it." (*Network*)

6. "Mrs. Robinson you're trying to illegally seduce a minor, aren't you?" (*The Graduate*)

5. "You want the truth? Okay, I'll give it to you." (*A Few Good Men*)

4. "I'll be back -- right after I get some groceries and pick up my dry cleaning." (*The Terminator*)

3. "Frankly, my dear, that's just what I was thinking." (*Gone With the Wind*)

2. "To hell with the bigger boat. Just take me back to shore." (*Jaws*)

1. "Rosebud -- my beloved childhood sled!" (*Citizen Kane*)

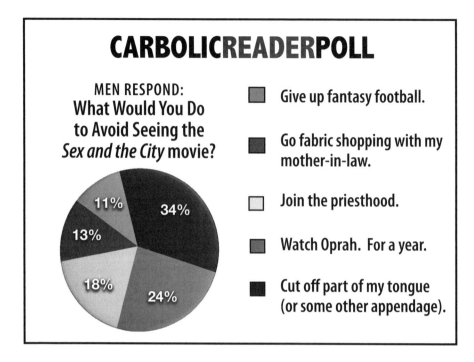

CARBOLICREADERPOLL

MEN RESPOND:
What Would You Do to Avoid Seeing the *Sex and the City* movie?

- Give up fantasy football.
- Go fabric shopping with my mother-in-law.
- Join the priesthood.
- Watch Oprah. For a year.
- Cut off part of my tongue (or some other appendage).

11% 34% 13% 18% 24%

WHAT I'M THANKFUL FOR THIS HOLIDAY SEASON: THAT OUR SKIN ISN'T MADE OF SPONGE MATERIAL WHEN IT RAINS

Commentary by Dr. Noah Swayne, Carbolic Science Analyst

Have you ever thought about how lucky we are to have skin? I mean from a SCIENTIFIC perspective?

Have you ever considered what would happen if our bodies were covered with sponge-like material instead? Well, I have.

In a heavy rain, our bodies would absorb so much water that our weight would nearly double. We would collapse on the floor, immobilized in a wet puddle due to the added weight. In cold temperatures, our puddle selves would freeze.

We would need to get a (dried out) person to squeeze the water out of us (and/or defrost us) just so we could stand up and walk around the room.

So the next time someone suggests it would be "better" if our bodies were covered with sponge material instead of skin, just point out these simple SCIENTIFIC facts.

CARBOLIC ASSASSINATION REVIEW: BENAZIR BHUTTO SHOOTING WAS DEAD-ON AND PISTOL-PERFECT

Sara Jane Moore, Freshly Paroled Carbolic Assassination Analyst

The killing of former Pakistan Prime Minister Benazir Bhutto was really a picture perfect, dead-on execution (excuse the multiple puns!). A gunman positioned himself in just the right spot at just the right time. Tucked away in the crowd, he stood behind and to the left of the vehicle carrying Bhutto when he fired three shots at her with a pistol.

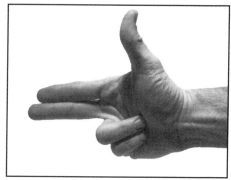

His aim was perfect. He properly waited to raise the gun until the right moment when he was ready to take his shot.

What struck me about the shooting was the preparation and the planning. This was not something that someone does by waking up that day and saying, "I think I'll shoot the former Prime Minister today." No, this effort clearly entailed many long hours of training and planning.

From a technical perspective, I give this assassination FOUR GUNS.

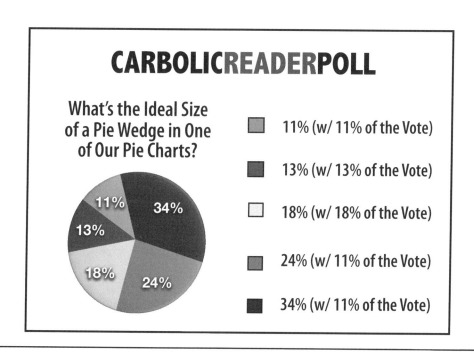

CARBOLICREADERPOLL

What's the Ideal Size of a Pie Wedge in One of Our Pie Charts?

- 11% (w/ 11% of the Vote)
- 13% (w/ 13% of the Vote)
- 18% (w/ 18% of the Vote)
- 24% (w/ 11% of the Vote)
- 34% (w/ 11% of the Vote)

JESSE JACKSON'S PROPOSAL TO CUT OFF SEN. OBAMA'S TESTICLES MAY GO TOO FAR

Commentary by Carbolic Smoke Editor, The Honorable Rufus Peckham

The Rev. Jesse Jackson has been a titan in the American sociopolitical milieu for forty years. Like every titan, he's beset with sneering, green-eyed troublemakers whose sole mission in life is to destroy him.

Take, for example, the whiners who bellyache that, contrary to Rev. Jackson's claims, he wasn't on the balcony with Dr. Martin Luther King when Dr. King was shot. And this is a big deal – exactly why?

So, it slipped Jackson's mind that he wasn't on the balcony -- sue him! Things slip my mind every day. Just yesterday I forgot to put out the trash and the recycling bin. So, you see, being on the balcony with the era's leading civil rights leader at the time he was shot - or not being on the balcony - is not the sort of thing one would necessarily remember. As I always say: If forgetfulness were a crime, the jails would be filled with senior citizens, and prison rape would be a thing of the past.

Or take the knee-jerk reaction of hyper-sensitive Jews who assumed Rev. Jackson must have been ridiculing the Jewish people when he called New York City "Hymietown." In point of fact, Hymietown is still listed on the books as the official name of one of the boroughs of New York – Manhattan, Queens, Brooklyn, and Hymietown. Far from ridiculing Jews, Rev. Jackson was, in fact, paying them homage.

Do you have any other pejorative allegations about Rev. Jackson? Bring 'em on, and I'll obliterate them one by one with the same unassailable logic. Rev. Jackson is a titan, plain and simple.

Of course, every now and again, even titans nod off.

That's what happened last week when Rev. Jackson was caught on a live microphone calling for Barack Obama's genital mutilation: "See, Barack's been talking down to black people . . . I want to cut his nuts off," Jackson said.

Before I proceed, I apologize to our female readers for using that crude description of a male body part, "nuts." (I can't believe it -- I just used that crude term again!) Truth be told, men discuss **(cont. on p. 167)**

PECKHAM: REV. JACKSON'S NUT-CUTTING PROPOSAL MAY GO TOO FAR

(cont. from p. 166) testicles in virtually every conversation we have with other men. Such as, "Hi, Jacob, are your chicken nuggets still sagging like they were in the locker room?" Or, "Gee, Adam, your chin ornaments are bulging through your shorts – and you ought to be really proud!" Or, "Pardon me, Brad, while I reach down and scratch my giggle berries."

Men limit their usage of testicular euphemisms to discussions with other men, because they realize women find this anatomical appendage at least mildly grotesque, and more fitting for a farm animal than a human being. We still don't know why this is. Perhaps if we could get a better look at them...

But I digress.

Getting back to Rev. Jackson: as much as I admire all that he's accomplished, whatever that might be, and as amusing as his comment was (since it involved testicles and all), after considerable reflection, I part company with him on castrating Senator Obama. For now.

At present, I would reserve the forced removal of testicles to animals and men who commit rape. Of course, by that same token, women who falsely accuse males of rape should have their tongues ripped out. (You see, my methods would promote a very healthy respect between the sexes — girls and boys would be scared to death to go near one another. And that's the way it should be.)

I do give Rev. Jackson credit for proposing an intriguing idea that merits serious public discourse: if someone says something you don't like, his balls are cut off. The genius of the plan is in its simplicity. And I am this close (putting index finger and thumb apart about an inch) to jumping on Rev. Jackson's bandwagon on this issue. But ultimately, his proposal suffers from overbreadth because it fails to set forth criteria to determine which sorts of comments merit turning a man into a eunuch.

It also suffers from an unfortunate gender asymmetry, because it provides no comparable mutilation for women. So it's back to the drawing board, Rev. Jackson. Once you come up with a more narrowly tailored plan to address these concerns, I am certain it will garner wide support.

Until then, Sen. Obama, your love apples are safe.

CARBOLIC FLASHBACK: MAY 26TH, 2005: "OH, THE SHAME OF THE BEETLE BAILEY PORN SCANDAL!"

Commentary by Carbolic Smoke Ball Editor, The Honorable Rufus Peckham

PITTSBURGH - We are aghast to report that last Sunday's edition of the venerable comic strip "Beetle Bailey" invented an appalling new dictionary entry for the word "depravity." It contains a panel that unabashedly flaunts the stark, flesh-tone image of an unclad Private Bailey. This decadence was disguised as the supposedly humorous depiction of the well-known soldier slipping in the shower. The Army hat adorning Beetle only served to crank up the kinkiness factor.

We have long celebrated "Beetle Bailey's" creator, Mort Walker, not only as a comic genius on a par with Mark Twain and S.J. Perelman but also as a patriot and, therefore, presumably a good Protestant and Republican. We are, therefore, crestfallen to find him wallowing in the same cesspool as Larry Flynt.

With no offense to our gay readers, this strip's sexual orientation has always been consonant with the American majority's, given General Halftrack's unrestrained lechery directed toward Miss Buxley. For millions of us, the General's heterosexual hijinks -- albeit degrading to women -- only underscored that the antics of the Camp Swampy gang were wholly suitable for a family audience. All that changed when Mr. Walker constructed a de facto shrine to an *au naturel* Beetle -- and there wasn't a female in sight.

Perhaps this sort of thing plays well at the Andy Warhol Museum, but it doesn't go over in the back of the Assembly Church where, because of Mr. Walker, the stacks of newspapers being hawked after Sunday services have become near-occasions of sin.

PEOPLE WON'T COME DOWNTOWN ANYMORE WITH THE VETERANS' DAY PARADE CLUTTERING UP OUR STREETS

Commentary by Ryan Kidd, Carbolic Teen Critic

Is it, like, any wonder people don't come downtown anymore, dude?

It seems like every year around Veterans Day, the dilapidated, ratty-looking war veterans of yore gimp along Fifth Avenue, cluttering up our streets with their war-mongering nostalgia and so forth. Thus was it so today as Pittsburgh observed yet another Veterans Day parade. Like, yawn!

These old men all act like they're still injured or wounded or not right in the head in their wheelchairs, some of them. Others, they walk upright carrying flags and what-not, looking altogether too proud of themselves, for whatever reason, with their medals pinned all over their old-man shirts.

Seriously, dude, is this the kind of people we want hanging around downtown? What kind of Velcro-sneaker, retirement-community-image are we trying to foster here? If our town father-dudes really want downtown to rock, they'll have to sponsor a video game parade or something, with hot chicks and beer. Then maybe we'll attract the right kind of people downtown.

THELASTWORD

THE PROLIFERATION OF "HUMOR" BOOKS IS IRREFUTABLE PROOF OF A CIVILIZATION IN FREE FALL

Commentary by Carbolic Smoke Ball Founder Emeritus, The Honorable Rufus Peckham

There is no more accurate barometer signaling a nation's decline than the insidious, creeping spread of the "Humor" sections of its bookstores.

I am heartsick to report that the unmistakable proliferation of "humor" books being peddled to our youth heralds nothing less than the annihilation of Western Civilization as we know it.

Every generation since the invention of the printing press has diligently read books so they could make the world better. Until now. For the first time, we have unwittingly spawned a generation of nitwits who diligently read books so they can *mock* and *scorn* and *deride* the world better.

These vile tomes typically share certain despicable traits. With cookie-cutter redundancy, they lambaste authority figures – including our own beloved President – by concocting all manner of preposterous artifice without discernible purpose, much less comedic effect. I suppose it makes the smug writers feel "good" about their sniveling, green-eyed selves to skewer persons who actually do things for mankind besides mindlessly ridiculing others.

Further, these books routinely sprinkle their inane blather with contemptible references to vaginas, penises and even the ejaculatory phenomena, subjects that should not be alluded to outside of their proper context – porno films and Milan Kundera novels.

I have spent considerable time searching these books for even a whiff of a redeeming quality. Sadly, I have found none. Certainly not the putative "humor"; nor the stilted and pompous prose; nor the pedestrian design; nor the egregiously inflated prices.

In short, these books disgrace our nation and defile our culture. I cannot fathom a single plausible reason for not burning each and every one of them.

And you read it here first.

CARBOLICSMOKEBALL

presents

ZOMBIES ATE MY END MATTER

CARBOLICSMOKEBALL IS ...

TIMMURRAY
Founder. Editor-in-Chief. Head Writer. Spiritual Advisor.

CHADHERMANN
Editorial Director. Writer. Communication Guru. Second Guitarist.

BOBHAAS
Co-Creator. Writer. Editor. Radio Personality.

NEALROSENBLAT
Staff Writer. Web Designer. Photographer.

SEANCANNON
Ace Reporter. Chief Investigator. Third Rail.

TIMOTHYSTEFKO
Cover Artist. Illustrator. Cool Dude.

SCOTTBROWN
Radio Personality. Steadfast Supporter.

TODDSHAFFER
Freelancer. Fourth-Chair Photoshopper.

CARBOLICSMOKEBALL debuted to almost universal critical indifference in July 2005. A little more than three years (and three thousand posts) later, our tireless dedication to news unencumbered by the facts has earned us a happily cult-like following, a mention in *The New York Times*, a weekly feature in the *Pittsburgh Tribune-Review*'s p.m. edition, and a weekly report on Pittsburgh's #1 radio station, 102.5 WDVE. After we finish our book tour, we'd like to open for Green Day. Or the Dalai Lama.

LEFTPAGEBLANK

Because you deserve a break. You've read an awful lot by now, and your sides probably hurt from laughing. We're just thinking of you and your health. Plus, we thought it would look cool. And we needed another page.

NOTES

Yeah, we know you don't need any, and we can't begin to imagine what you'd write after reading this book -- except, perhaps, for anonymous emails of outrage -- but we thought it would make us seem nice. And smart.

CARBOLICSPECIALTHANKS

Mort Walker and Mike Madison, each in their own ways, for jump-starting it all.

Peter Leo, who discovered us, championed us, and delivered us from total obscurity to a pleasant, comfortable state of semi-obscurity.

Randy Baumann, Jim Krenn, Ryan Caruso, Sean McDowell, Val Porter, Mike Prisuta, and everyone else at WDVE for loyal support and primo air time.

Frank Craig, Jim Cuddy, Chris Pastrick, and the *Pittsburgh Tribune-Review* crew for taking a chance on fake news in a real newspaper, then making us look so darned good every Monday *p.m.*

Brian O'Neill -- who wrote about us, and even told *The New York Times* about us -- and Dennis Roddy and the rest of our early adopters at the *Pittsburgh Post-Gazette*.

Chris Potter, Chris Young, and the other fine folks at *Pittsburgh City Paper*.

The great Mike Woycheck, the incomparable PittGirl, the lovely Sherry, and all the rest of our favorite, faithful supporters in the Burghosphere.

Rick Sebak, for his too-kind introduction, and for supporting us from not long after the beginning.

The good folks and photographers of Stock.Xchng for plentiful resources from which we could legally replace all the photos and images we'd previously ~~pilfered~~ ~~borrowed~~ liberated for use on the web site.

Dave Nolfi, who gave our co-creators their start doing fake news on Dynamic CableVision in Homestead, Pennsylvania, way back in 1973. He helped to nurture the seeds of Carbolic long before anyone ever gave any thought to planting an *Onion*.

Professor Emcee Square, for bringing Carbolic *Alive* on TV in his own, inimitably undead way.

Ian Urbina of *The New York Times*, for getting us on the front page and the fast track to credibility.

Jon Delano, Dan Onorato, Jack Bogut, Bob Mayo, John McIntire, Selena Zito, Josie Roberts, Eric Heyl, and Dr. Thomas Starzl, for quoting us and writing about us and supporting us in ways we'll always appreciate. And won't ever forget.

CARBOLICSPECIALTHANKS

The whole host of occasional Carbolic correspondents and contributors -- including Mike Giunta, Char, Liz Dolinar, John Lewis, Bill Kennedy, and Scotty "The Mayor" Brown -- who've helped us bring the funny.

Martin Jasmin, Karine McMahon, and everyone at Transcontinental Printing, Jim O'Brien, The Bowker Bunch, Gary Morton, and everyone at Renaissance News for getting this book into your hands.

Kim Brown, Ron and Patty Jones, Rep. Jesse White, for help and support.

Fox's Pizza in Baldwin, PA; Dave's Terrace Bakery in Whitehall, PA; Villa Reale Pizza, Monticello's Pizza, Fuel and Fuddle, Gullifty's, Max & Erma's, and Joe's Dog House in Pittsburgh, PA.

Patti Cannon, Ellie Valecko, Andy Newman, Donna Reich, Claudia Stolz, Brother Holloway, Sister Antonio, Mike Maloney, Steve Schain, and especially Mom and Dad Cannon, for the support.

Meryl Sustarsic, Mom Welsh, and Poppa Rosenblat.

Judith Stefko, and Lindsay and Jason Stefko, for understanding where Dad was and what he was doing.

Jewel & Vince Haas. Bill & Tom Haas. Mary Ann Blank. Rose D'Orazio & Vince Haas. Doe Doe. Jean & Dick Dobos. Jim Hannigan, Bob Russo, and Fr. Dave Crowley.

Wendy, Adam, and Ethan Hermann for understanding and inspiring. Ron Vassel, Jim Pascoe, and Nitya Venkataraman for empowering. Ruth Lombardo for loving. Beth and Rod Hermann for everything.

Dr. John Murray, Liz Murray ("The Duke"), and Jacqueline Murray. Susan Cabin, Jon Hogue, and James A. Mollica, Jr.   What's left of The Hon. John Patrick Hester. Jan "The Man." Anita and Brian Starceski. Msgr. Henry Immekus.

Anyone and everyone we forgot. (If you're upset, we understand, and we're sorry. If you're happy, because you'd rather not be associated with us, we *really* understand. And you're welcome.)

And, finally, all our wonderful fans, readers, viewers, web surfers, and unsuspecting bookstore browsers. We like to make ourselves laugh, but we're still sort of astonished that we make you laugh too. Thanks for that. For indulging us. And for helping, all those late nights and early mornings, to keep us going.

ABOUT THE BOOK

Zombies Ate My Headlines was set in multiple variations of the Myriad Pro font, with some titles and accents set in 3rd Man. The Carbolic Smoke Ball wordmark and all similar titles were set in Abadi MT Condensed.

The book was laid out and designed on an Apple Power Mac, using Pages, Preview, Numbers, and Safari, as well as Adobe Photoshop and Microsoft Word, viewed on a 23" Apple Cinema Display, while listening to a little Bruce Springsteen and a whole lot of Drive-By Truckers.

The front and back covers were conceived by Chad Hermann and (brilliantly) executed by Timothy Stefko, whose mad genius also produced the title-page sketches and the *Zombies* title-logo design.

Photo credits go to Tim Murray, Neal Rosenblat, Chad Hermann, and several dozen digital artists whose work can be seen, admired, downloaded, and purchased at sxc.hu. A few photos come from wire services and archival sources, but they have been subject to manipulations and absurdifications that render them satirical fair game. Credit for manipulating and absurdifying those photos goes to Tim Murray, Todd Shaffer, Neal Rosenblat, and Chad Hermann. Neal gets extra credit for the Venus de Milo's breast enhancement.

The book was printed and bound by Transcontinental Printing in Louiseville, Quebec, under the watchful eye and steady hand of Karine McMahon, and then distributed by Renaissance News, Inc.

Zombies Ate My Headlines, like all great social satire that includes the living dead, proudly hails from the hills and rivers and occasionally indelicate sensibilities of Pittsburgh, Pennsylvania.

INMEMORIAM

OBITUARY: THE HON. RUFUS PECKHAM: JURIST, EDITOR, *BON VIVANT*; ADVOCATE OF THE WORLD'S DOWNTRODDEN

THE HON. RUFUS PECKHAM, *BON VIVANT* AND CRUSADING JURIST whose legal philosophy was so advanced that even he could not fully comprehend it, died unexpectedly last night.

"He was the most frightening individual I've ever met in my life. A real nasty son-of-a-bitch. But I mean that in a good way," said Judge Peckham's long-time associate Noah Swayne.

Peckham was born in Johnstown, Pennsylvania, on the day of the great flood in 1936. "My mother's water broke while she was walking down the street," the Judge once said, "so I've always blamed her for all the deaths and destruction."

After graduating law school, his fledgling law practice struggled. "It was either get elected judge or steal the money I was holding for my clients in trust," the Judge told a New York Times reporter in 2006. "I still wonder about what might have been."

While serving on the Pennsylvania Court of Appeals, he sentenced sixteen men to death, all for breach of contract cases.

Well-known for his tireless, civic-minded efforts, Judge Peckham became a crusader for women's rights. He still holds the record for the most money raised in one day to buy breast implants for impoverished third world women. "Women everywhere should have the right to control their oppressor males by flaunting their enormous, shapely breasts," he proudly explained. "And some of those impoverished women are really hot."

The Judge's celebrated feud with variety show host Ed Sullivan made headlines after Sullivan banned him from his Sunday night show. The feud started when Sullivan claimed that the Judge exposed himself during a televised monologue. The Judge always insisted that Sullivan's eyes deceived him. "I was merely holding [Mexican mouse-puppet] Topo Gigio near my crotch," the Judge explained.

The Judge was allegedly distraught in the days leading up to his death after learning that every news story reported by the news outlet he founded, Carbolic Smoke Ball, turned out to be fake. Father Samuel Blatchford of Saint Rosacea of Blawnox spoke about (cont. on p. 181)

RESTINPECKHAM

OUR EDITOR: JURIST, *BON VIVANT*, ADVOCATE OF THE WORLD'S DOWNTRODDEN

(cont. from p. 180) THE JUDGE'S DEATH: "Persons who suffer from dementia simply are not, in the eyes of the Lord, deemed responsible for their actions." Asked to explain what he meant, Father Blatchford merely sighed.

The Judge is survived by his fifth wife, Velveeta Lugosi-Peckham, and three children, who agreed to be mentioned on condition of anonymity.

In accordance with his wishes, and in imitation of his lifelong hero, Benito Mussolini, the Judge's body will be hung upside down on a meat hook tonight. Tomorrow his head will be paraded around the town square on a stick. A public viewing of the rest of his body will be held at the Pleasant Hills Public Library tomorrow from 2-4 and 7-9. On Monday, a memorial will be erected in his honor. Burial will be private -- no other bodies will be buried with him.

Donations in lieu of flowers can be made to the International Breast Implant Society.